Included and Valued

Langham

GLOBAL LIBRARY

Since I first entered into advocacy for disability issues in Tanzania and globally, I have read a lot of books concerning disability issues. Many books have been written from all over the world, including some from Africa. However, in all those years I have never come across a book on disability written from a religious perspective. While I was working with the Free Pentecostal Church of Tanzania (FPCT), I influenced the church to have a "Church Disability Policy" which was approved in 2009. Many theologians have viewed persons with disabilities as a charity model, that is, people to be pitied and given services in order to receive blessings from God.

Included and Valued has a different perspective, viewing disability from an inclusive standpoint whereby persons with disability are given the opportunity to serve God just like every other person in the community where they live. While reading this book I was so fascinated, especially with the explanation about disability and persons with disabilities. It is my belief that this book will open more doors for people with disabilities to be included in various aspects in the church. I recommend this book to religious leaders and church members as it will change the mindset of the community towards persons with disabilities. According to the Bible, God created human beings in his image. Therefore, persons with disabilities are people created by God to serve him and not to be pitied and regarded as people to facilitate others to be blessed by God through their charity! Disability therefore should be looked upon as a human and development issue!

As is well known, religious leaders have the power to change people's attitudes, so this book will facilitate the change of attitudes of the community towards persons with disabilities.

Josephat Torner
Co-founder and CEO, Josephat Torner Foundation
Advocate for persons with Albinism

This is a supremely practical book, which confronts so many of the myths surrounding disability in all its forms. It is written by actual practitioners who have dedicated their lives to working with the disabled in their communities here on the continent of Africa. At its heart, this book is a clarion call for inclusivity, for all of us, of all faiths and backgrounds, to recognize the absolute humanity and divinity in each and every one of us. In the eyes and loving hands of God, we are all equal, regardless of our physical, cultural and ethnic attributes. This book shines with a light of understanding and hope, dispelling the darkness of prejudice and exclusion. This is not a book to sit cleanly on a shelf, but rather is a guide which demands to travel with us, as we go out to our communities to conduct outreach on hot afternoons under the shade of a mango tree. This book should accompany us not just to the villages and small towns, but also to the great urban centres of Africa, where the disabled are too often lost in the melee of the city. Over time, the pages should become sullied with the dust of the land, bearing witness to the fact that it has been our companion along the way.

"For we are his workmanship, created in Christ Jesus for good works, which God prepared beforehand, that we should walk in them." Ephesians 2:10

Friar Giannone Carmelo
Minister Provincial,
Order of Friars Minor (OFM),
Province of St Francis in East Africa, Madagascar and Mauritius

Bridget Hathaway and Flavian Kishekwa have taken a huge effort to research one of the most neglected areas in African writings. The result is a very rich, informative and compelling argument for us to consider how African communities and families treat our sisters and brothers living with all kinds of disabilities. Their research is littered with people's stories and anecdotes, local beliefs and practices, and how they impact everyday African life. The ecology of meanings in these pages integrates a robust engagement with challenging Bible texts and a wealth of theological scholarship. Bridget and Flavian do not shy away from tackling difficult questions such as how we relate to the theme of suffering alongside our belief in an almighty God, and what it means to be human when one is disabled. This is a must-read resource for both academics and practitioners considering working with vulnerable people in an African context or anybody motivated by intellectual curiosity to understand issues surrounding disability in Africa. Read this book and learn from those who have lived and worked close to where it hurts.

Rev Paul Nzacahayo, PhD
Methodist Minister
Tutor,
Queen's Foundation for Ecumenical Theological Education, Birmingham, UK

Included and Valued

A Practical Theology of Disability

Bridget Hathaway and Flavian Kishekwa

Langham
GLOBAL LIBRARY

This book is dedicated to all people living with disability who have been marginalized from society and have been denied the opportunity to be part of the life and work of the community and the church. May they be given their right to express and use their gifts in the life of their communities, places of worship and society in general.

CONTENTS

List of Figures

Foreword

The kingdom of God is far greater than we can imagine. Jesus's ministry shows us that it is a realm full of surprises, not least the inclusion of those whom the world discards or ignores. He had his eye on widows, children, the blind, the lame, the sick and the destitute. From those in church and secular power today, riding the success of their own achievements, he expects the same Christ-like attention to those who are at the margins.

Bridget Hathaway and Flavian Kishekwa's compelling narrative not only gives parity of esteem to those labelled casually, "disabled," but also asserts that being vulnerable to the vulnerable gives to leaders a profound experience of compassion and healing graced by the Holy Spirit. Inclusion of those with disability brings gifts of transformed power and a more authentic church.

Included and Valued weaves together the practical and the theological, drawing constantly on the Bible and on social and professional insights to encourage the pastor and others to have care and confidence amongst those with disability.

This profoundly hopeful book is rich in straightforward, useful advice. Its clear descriptions and illustrations of often bewildering conditions will repay careful study by those Christians who are trying to come alongside. From physical and mental impairments to psychiatric disorders and sensory distortions the author tackles assumptions about pastoral practice, spiritual truth, healing, abuse and social taboos.

Physical, mental or sensory disability can be cruel and painful. It can be unwanted by the person experiencing it, or their family or their community. But many with disability know that they are made in the image of God, with a vocation to Christian fullness of life. They praise, evangelize, encourage and care. They minster joyfully, both to those around them and to confident young visitors from far-flung lands.

My own calling to follow the Lord Jesus was in such circumstances, working in southwest Uganda as an eighteen year old amongst the Christian disabled of a UN/CMS sponsored Rural Rehabilitation Centre on Bwama Island. Whether through the warm smile from Richard who looked up from the ground to welcome me, my humbling as an incompetent dugout canoeist, or by being outplayed on a soccer pitch by an opponent who pivoted on a stick to score right past me, my childhood Bible-knowledge and youthful self-assurance was converted into a maturing trust in Jesus Christ as Saviour and Lord.

I am grateful for a timely reminder that life with the disabled is a gift and a joy, a full expression of discipleship together, worshipping the King in whom "all the fullness of God was pleased to dwell, and through him to reconcile himself to all things, whether on earth or in heaven, making peace by the blood of his cross" (Col 1:18–19).

As we absorb the implications of the authors' prophetic study for our own ministries, let us keep in mind the words of Dietrich Bonhoeffer quoted by Ray McCloughry on page 90 of this book: "There is no worthless life before God, because God holds life itself to be valuable." And let us respond even more deeply to the grace and command of Lord Jesus: "Love one another as I have loved you" (John 15:12 ESV).

The Rt Rev David Urquhart
Bishop of Birmingham, UK

Acknowledgments

Writing a book requires a lot of team work, and this book is no exception. We are both very grateful for the amount of support we received as we tackled the various challenges we faced in completing this handbook. Without the encouragement of many people we might not have finished the project.

It is not possible to mention everyone by name because that would take several pages. However, there are a few individuals and groups we must mention as they have played a key part in enabling us to reach this final stage.

The Anglican Diocese of Kagera, Tanzania, has supported the concept of Community Based Rehabilitation (CBR) since 1994. We are thankful for their continued support of Karagwe Community Based Rehabilitation Programme (KCBRP) since its beginning in 2003; Flavian has a leadership role within this programme, which is now known as Community Based Inclusive Development Organisation – Kagera. We are especially grateful to Rev Canon Aggrey Mashanda, Executive Director, and the staff who have allowed Flavian time to work on the book.

We are grateful to Crosslinks for their understanding and support in allowing Bridget the time to co-author the book. We greatly appreciate the way Bridget's individual supporters and Link Churches have joined this venture in both prayer and financial assistance. To Mary we say a special "thank you" for her generosity that enabled Flavian and Bridget to meet together in Tanzania so we could write together, side by side at the same table!

The second section of the handbook required much research, thought and background reading. Bridget could not have done this without the facilities of the library at Queen's Foundation for Ecumenical Theological Education in Birmingham, UK. There she found a well-stocked library that is conducive to study! Thanks, too, to Andrea, Evelyn and Theresa for their friendship, challenging discussions and encouragement.

We are thrilled that St Peter's Church, Kayanga, Kagera, Tanzania, has embraced the inclusion concept and is now a fine example of a church striving to be inclusive of people with disability. We say "thank you" to Rev Canon Naftal Hosea for beginning to bring our book to life right here in Karagwe. We are also grateful for his help with information for the chapter on beliefs and attitudes.

xvi   Included and Valued

We are grateful that Langham Publishing realized the importance of a book on the subject of disability and theology in an African context. We are thankful for all the help and encouragement they gave us during the writing of it.

This book would not exist without all those people living with disability, and their families, carers and friends, who have taught us so much and agreed to our using some of their stories and photographs in this handbook. May God's blessing and encouragement rest with all of them.

General Introduction

When people talk about disability or they meet someone with a disability, their attitude is often dependent on their culture, their spiritual beliefs and their previous experience regarding disability. Unfortunately, a negative attitude to disability is not unusual, and from Bible times onwards we know that people with disability have largely faced discrimination, often being denied their basic human rights. The wider church is not innocent with regard to discrimination, even if it is not intentional. The purpose of this handbook is therefore to help those who are involved in church leadership to understand more about disability, to assist them in exploring Bible passages regarding various aspects of disability and to provide practical ideas that will enable them to lead a disability-friendly church. Disability is not the result of sin; people with disability are made in the image of God like everyone else, and for that very reason are a part of the church family and community. It is hoped that this handbook will lead to a change in attitude towards people with disability by those in church leadership, and that this will extend out to the wider community.

There are a number of books available concerning disability in an African context; however, there are fewer books that look at disability from a theological perspective. In a continent where belief in the spirit world remains active, it is important to ensure that the Holy Spirit is the basis of our beliefs in the church. This is not to deny the presence of evil spirits, but to acknowledge that the victory over evil was won on the cross at Calvary. A lack of understanding or knowledge about disability can lead to acceptance of harmful traditional beliefs. It is hoped that this book will, at least in part, provide the tools to enable those in church leadership to combat these beliefs with biblical truth.

The subject of disability often raises much discussion regarding terminology. The different ideas regarding what is correct terminology can create difficulty in knowing which terms to use; indeed, people living with disability themselves may, for example, use the term "disabled person" when those without disability avoid it. In this handbook we have sometimes used the term "impairment," at other times "disability," and on occasion "people living with disability." We are aware that the terms "disability" and "impairment" can hold different meanings, but bearing in mind the challenges of translation we decided to use the terms interchangeably to avoid misunderstanding. The

New International Version (2011) of the Holy Bible has been used throughout unless stated otherwise.

Section I of the handbook explains about several types of disability and their causes and looks briefly at how they can be managed, with the aim of reducing harmful beliefs, some of which are recorded. Unfortunately, this book allows for only the briefest of explanations; there is much more to be said about the types of disability mentioned, and other disabilities are not included. We would urge readers to explore these issues further by using books and websites.

In the second section, such subjects as being made in the image of God, what it means to be human, and disability and healing are looked at from a theological perspective. It is not possible to cover every viewpoint in a book, but throughout we have aimed to inform as well as challenge readers to think more deeply about the complexity of disability issues.

The third section motivates people to realize the abilities of people with disability in the context of the church. The objective in this section is to encourage and enable church leaders to create an environment where greater active inclusion of people with disability in church and community life can take place. We realize this may be challenging for many reasons, but even the smallest attempt brings the church closer to the pattern that Jesus taught. In the following quotation we could also add "people with disability or without disability":

> So in Christ Jesus you are all children of God through faith, for all of you who were baptised into Christ have clothed yourselves with Christ. There is neither Jew nor Gentile, neither slave nor free, nor is there male and female, for you are all one in Christ Jesus. (Gal 3:26–28)

Section I

Understanding Disability Is Important

1

Introduction to Disability

People living with disability face significant social challenges. They experience discrimination and stigma, and consequently are often invisible in society; this hampers full participation in the lives of their families and communities. The presence of superstitious beliefs about disability amongst communities across the world, such as that being disabled is an outcome of past wrongdoing, undermines the capacity of people with disability to be valued and respected members of society. In many places they are kept indoors; this prevents them from accessing quality education and from participating in social and economic activities.

People with disability also face substantial limitations due to environmental barriers. Adjustments in infrastructure would create wider opportunities for people with disability to effectively participate in the community. Although these improvements would significantly reduce dependency and limitations, especially for people with moderate disability conditions, those who are more profoundly disabled would remain severely restricted.

When people have little understanding of disability, they often search for the cause; lacking scientific knowledge, many people turn to traditional beliefs as an answer. Sadly, a mixture of fear and misunderstanding may result in harmful practices being carried out against people with disability, as well as the marginalization of entire families. It is hoped that the chapters in this section will help to dispel some of the myths about disability.

What Do We Mean by "People with Disability"?

The term "people with disability" refers to people who have lasting physical, intellectual, sensory and psychiatric/mental impairments. Some types of disability may be invisible; for example, conditions which are related to psychiatric disorders and some types of learning difficulties are sometimes hidden. Never assume that someone has no disability just because it is not apparent.

How People Perceive Disability

People have different perceptions about disability depending on their context. For example, people living in rural areas may have different ideas about disability from those living in large towns or cities. In order for us to understand the term "disability," we first need to be able to differentiate it from other conditions that are habitually confused with disability. The most common error is to equate disability with disease or illness. However, although diseases may cause disability and, conversely, some disability conditions cause a person to be more vulnerable to certain diseases, disability itself is a lifelong condition, unlike most illnesses.

A Concept of "Disability"

Disability is a permanent or progressive condition that interferes with an individual's performance in day-to-day activities. It is characterized by cognitive, neurological, sensory or physical impairment, or a combination of these impairments. A person with disability essentially faces limitations in performing certain functions when compared with people with no disability. For example, disability may affect a person's capacity in learning, mobility, communication and interaction with other people. Some people may face all these challenges. Disability may arise at any time in a person's life: some people are born with disability, while others acquire disability sometime during their lives. Sometimes we know the cause of the disability, but other times the cause is unknown. Disability can affect any person, irrespective of age or ethnicity. As the World Health Organization says: "Disability is a complex phenomenon, reflecting an interaction between features of a person's body and features of the society in which he or she lives."[1]

The Accident

The following story explores understandings of the term "disability."

---

1. Quoted at "Definitions of Disability," Disabled World, accessed 8 August 2018, https://www.disabled-world.com/definitions/disability-definitions.php.

Paulo and Dominic were good friends; they were in the same class at school and lived in the same part of town. In fact, the teachers called them "two peas from the same pod" as they spent so much time together. Dominic loved playing football; in fact, the only time Paulo was separated from Dominic was when Dominic was playing, but Paulo would usually watch from the sidelines. "Come on, Dom!" Paulo would shout. "You're playing for both of us!" Of course, Paulo would love to have joined in, but his right leg had been damaged at birth, so it was weak and thin. He knew people called him "disabled" but he didn't really think of himself like that. He wouldn't get better, he knew that, but he still enjoyed life.

One day, Dominic was playing in a school match and the opposing team were bigger boys, quite aggressive in their play. Suddenly Dominic was tackled from behind and with a loud cry he fell to the ground. "Oh my leg!" he screamed. "It hurts, it hurts!" The referee stopped the game, and Dominic was carried off in agony. At the hospital the doctor said that his leg was badly broken and Dominic would be in plaster for six weeks. "And then you will need to use a crutch for another two weeks," the doctor added.

"Will I play football again?" Dominic asked the doctor, "or am I now disabled, like my friend Paulo?"

But Paulo was the one to answer: "Of course you're not disabled!" he laughed. "Well, only temporarily; but you will recover fully, not like me; mine is for life." And they laughed together, as friends do.

Was Paulo not able? Often people think that someone with a disability is unable to do much; even schooling is denied to many children with disability. In the story we read, "He [Paulo] knew people called him 'disabled' but he didn't really think of himself like that." Paulo was able to do everything except run and play football with his friend; he could play many other sports if given the opportunity, such as sitting volleyball and wheelchair tennis, which many able-bodied people cannot manage to play.

According to the International Classification of Impairments, Disabilities and Handicaps (ICIDH), "Disability discrimination is the act of treating someone with a disability less favorably than someone without a disability."[2] Perhaps many of us are guilty of discriminating against people with disability, not recognizing their abilities.

There has been much discussion in disability groups about the difference between medical and social models of disability. We cannot discuss these ideas in detail in this book, but the following explanation might be helpful. From a

---

2. Quoted at "Definitions of Disability."

medical perspective, disability is viewed as being the result of trauma, disease, genetics or illness, and as such requires medical intervention and supervision. From a social viewpoint, attitudes to people with disability affect their ability to be included in society, their human rights and their ability to access education and health care. Environmental accessibility may also have a major impact on the lives of people with disability.

Summary

As church leaders, our own attitude to disability may well influence the attitudes of others, and this is a big responsibility. May we all seek to be examples of inclusiveness rather than perpetuating the marginalizing attitude that is often found in our society.

2

Physical Disability

Physical disability is the more obvious type of disability because it is usually visible, affecting the limbs or trunk of a person's body. It involves abnormality of one or more parts of the body. The nervous system may also be involved, resulting in paralysis which impairs physical activities, including mobility. We will look at the causes of physical disability in this chapter. As we do so, we should remember that people with physical challenges encounter certain difficulties due to their disability; frequently, however, the limitations are due to society's attitude to disability rather than to the person's actual physical limitations. Physical barriers and negative social attitudes restrict the person's participation in community life, despite his or her desire to participate as fully as possible. Many people with disability long to live independently, although for some this will not be possible and they will depend on partial or permanent support.

General Causes of Physical Disability

Physical disability has several causes; it may be congenital (from birth), genetic (inherited) or a result of injury or serious disease; for example, a road accident may result in amputation of a limb or paralysis. Illnesses such as meningitis and cerebral malaria can cause permanent disability. Physical disability may also occur as a result of the ageing process; for example, as we get older, some parts of the body may become weak and less active, and some people may need walking aids to support them in their mobility.

What do we mean by genetic or inherited disability? This idea often causes people to blame others for the occurrence of a disability, but we should never blame anyone; this is not a godly attitude and it may have negative consequences, such as the break-up of a marriage. Usually a genetic disability is due to inheriting a malformed gene that carries a particular disorder, such as sickle cell anaemia, albinism or muscular dystrophy. This malformed gene is passed down through the family, usually to each generation. Sometimes it is a malformed chromosome that causes the disorder, as, for example, in Down's syndrome (see chapter 3 on intellectual impairment).

Looking in More Detail at Physical Disability

What might cause a congenital disability to occur? When a woman is pregnant there are certain medicines she should not use; this is why a medical practitioner will ask a woman if she is pregnant before prescribing medicines. The same applies to local medicine. Using these medicines can cause malformation of the foetus; in addition, excessive use of alcohol[1] or addictive drugs such as marijuana[2] can also be harmful to the baby.

Some disabilities are caused by the birth process. A pregnant woman may experience a prolonged or difficult labour followed by a slow birth; both baby and mother are tired, the first important cry of the baby is late, and this can result in lack of oxygen to the baby, resulting in damage to the brain. Children who are born very prematurely are also at a high risk of a variety of physical conditions due to incomplete development of their organs.

Immediately after birth or during the first year of life, a child is very vulnerable to infections. In poor environments where hygiene may be difficult, the child might become sick from an infection which, if not treated, can cause a disability. For example, if a boil or cut becomes infected, it can cause osteomyelitis, which is an infection that penetrates the bone and begins to destroy it. This can have very disabling consequences.

Some Common Physical Conditions We Might Meet

Cerebral Palsy

Cerebral palsy (CP) is a common physical condition in Africa that is caused by damage to the part of the brain that controls movement and coordination. In most cases the damage occurs during pregnancy or birth. However, damage

---

1. "Alcohol and Pregnancy" information sheet, Royal College of Obstetricians & Gynaecologists, accessed 6 September 2018, www.rcog.org.uk/globalassets/documents/patients/patient-information-leaflets/pregnancy/pi-alcohol-and-pregnancy.pdf.

2. Paul Taylor, "Will Smoking Marijuana During Pregnancy Harm the Child?," *Globe & Mail*, updated 5 June 2018, accessed 6 September 2018, https://www.theglobeandmail.com/life/health-and-fitness/health-advisor/will-smoking-marijuana-during-pregnancy-harm-the-child/article35982408/.

can sometimes occur in later life due to head injury or a serious illness that is connected to the brain, especially cerebral malaria and meningitis. Cerebral palsy can also affect speech, vision, hearing and understanding. In some cases the person with CP will also have epilepsy. When a part of the brain is damaged, it is difficult for it to recover fully; therefore a child with CP will live with the consequences for all of his or her life. Unfortunately, there is no medicine or injection that can cure CP. However, if there is early medical intervention there is a very good chance that the child will develop well, live a good life and be included in the community. Sometimes people with CP exhibit uncontrolled actions in their limbs, but all these movements are consequences of the brain damage; they are not related to witchcraft or evil spirits.

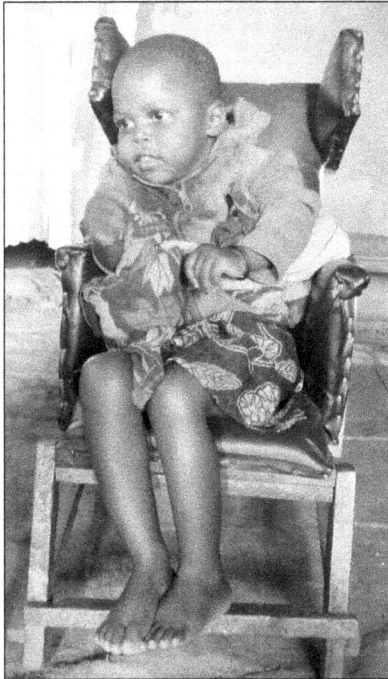

Figure 2.1. A young child with cerebral palsy.
Photo ©Bridget Hathaway.

The best way to help a child with CP is by consulting professionals, especially physiotherapists and occupational therapists, who can help the parents understand how to support their child.

What Causes Cerebral Palsy?

As mentioned above, CP is caused by damage to the brain that may happen before, during or just after birth, and even sometimes later in a child's life. Sometimes we do not know the real cause of CP, but the following gives some ideas about the causes.

Causes before Birth

Some people wonder how a child can acquire a disability before birth. However, the brain starts developing when the baby is still in the mother's womb; therefore a pregnant mother must guard her pregnancy carefully. The causes of CP include serious illness in the pregnant mother, such as measles; excessive use of alcohol and drugs can also cause CP. Some local medicines are harmful if taken during early pregnancy, so it is important for the pregnant woman to take only medicines that have been recommended by health professionals, for her own safety as well as for that of her unborn baby. Also, any accident affecting the womb of the pregnant woman, including a serious fall or being beaten, may lead to head injury in the unborn baby.

Causes during Birth

As stated above, a lack of oxygen to the baby's brain during a difficult delivery is a frequent cause of CP. Unsafe delivery environments may cause injury to the head of the baby at birth; for example, babies may hit their heads on a hard surface or be extracted from the womb by an unsafe method. A difficult delivery is more common in young mothers whose reproductive organs are not yet mature.

Causes after Birth

Brain infections such as meningitis or cerebral malaria can cause brain damage in the baby. CP can also be acquired after severe head injuries in a person of any age; a brain tumour may also cause damage to the brain.

Premature babies are at high risk of acquiring CP as their organs are not so well developed; they may have difficulties in breathing, which puts them at high risk of lack of oxygen to the brain after birth, with consequential brain damage. Other risk factors for CP include giving birth to twins, a very young mother (below eighteen years old) or an older mother (over forty years old). A baby with a low birth weight (less than 1 kg) is also at greater risk of having CP.

So Is There Just One Type of Cerebral Palsy?

There are three main types of CP. We will look at two types. The important thing, however, is not the names, but how the child is affected.

Spastic Cerebral Palsy

Spastic CP is the common type of CP that causes muscle stiffness of the limbs. Many children with spastic CP have mobility challenges because of uncontrolled and sudden muscle spasms. In addition, some children with spastic CP have problems with vision and epilepsy. Intellectual challenges may be present.

CP affects different parts of the body depending on the severity and which part of the brain is affected. It can affect the muscle movements of one side of the body (hemiplegia), lower limbs only (diplegia) or the entire body (quadriplegia). When the entire body is affected it is quite often difficult for a child to stand without support.

Figure 2.2. Israel's entire body is affected by CP.
Photo ©Bridget Hathaway.

Athetoid Cerebral Palsy

Children with athetoid CP face difficulties in controlling their body movements. The condition causes involuntary uncontrolled movements in the arms, legs, hands and face.

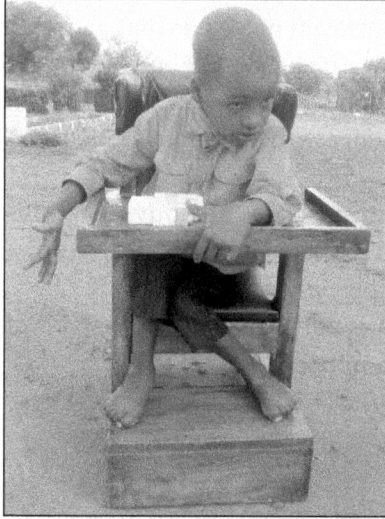

Figure 2.3. This child has athetoid CP. Photo ©Flavian Kishekwa.

The movements often become worse when the children are trying to do something or speak, or when they get upset or excited. Generally, these unwanted movements hinder an individual's performance in walking, sitting, swallowing and even talking. It should be noted that children with athetoid CP usually have good understanding like other children; just because they cannot talk well does not mean they don't understand. Children with athetoid CP should have the opportunity of being included in mainstream or special schooling where they are likely to achieve well.

Spina Bifida

Spina bifida means "split spine," or we could say "a split in the spine." It is a birth defect which happens a few weeks after conception whereby the tissues that come together to make the tube where the spinal cord runs do not close well. This allows the nerve to push out from the safety of the vertebra. When a nerve is exposed in this way it is easily damaged and can no longer take messages from the brain to the different parts of the body. The result is paralysis below the affected section of the spine.

The consequences of spina bifida vary depending on the type of defect, the size, and the place where the defect is located. Children with spina bifida may have partial or sometimes total lower-limb paralysis which affects bladder and bowel control. Frequently children with spina bifida also have hydrocephalus, which is when fluid in the brain fails to drain out, resulting in an enlarged head to accommodate the fluid (see below). It is a dangerous state which needs immediate medical attention.

Spina bifida is a serious condition because it affects the spine, and if spina bifida is suspected, any newborn baby should be sent to a specialist centre immediately. The opening in the spine leaves the main nerve uncovered, which increases the risk of infection. That infection could then be transferred to the brain, which would usually cause death.

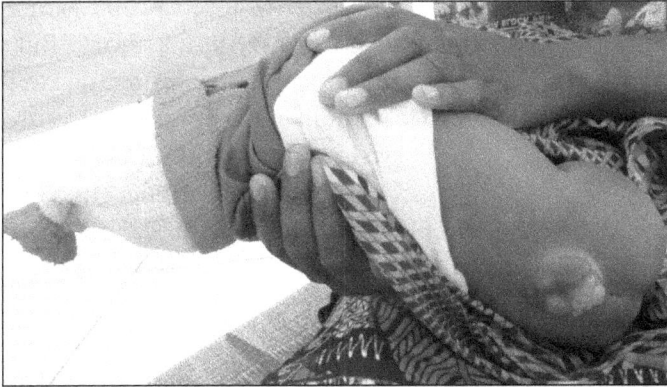

Figure 2.4. A newborn baby with spina bifida.
Photo ©Bridget Hathaway.

What Causes Spina Bifida?

The cause of spina bifida is largely unknown; some suggest that spina bifida may be connected to genetics or environmental factors, but at the moment no one is sure. It cannot be entirely prevented, but doctors do know that taking folic acid just before a pregnancy and during the first twelve weeks of pregnancy can reduce the risk of spina bifida. *It is therefore important to take folic acid in early pregnancy.* As pastors, advise the young women in your congregations to take folic acid when they become pregnant; this may prevent children being born with spina bifida.

Managing spina bifida correctly is important. In most cases of spina bifida, surgery is effective. Unfortunately, not every doctor can perform spina

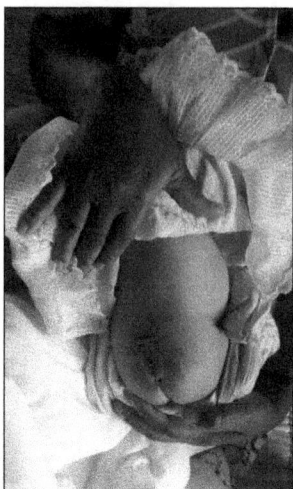

Figure 2.5. The previous newborn baby after surgery. Photo ©Flourian Protase. Used by permission.

bifida surgery; it needs specialized doctors who are normally found in referral hospitals. Importantly, the baby should be operated on within the first few days after birth; every day without treatment is a risk to the baby's life. We will not say more about management; this introduction to spina bifida is enough to help you understand a little more about this condition.

Hydrocephalus

Hydrocephalus simply means "water on the brain." When you see a child with a very large head it can give you a shock. But do not be afraid: the size of the head is due to there being a lot of fluid in the brain, which causes the brain to swell. If the condition is not well treated as early as possible, it can affect the child's physical and intellectual development. As noted above, hydrocephalus may also be a consequence of spina bifida.

The Normal Function of Fluid in the Brain

The brain is complicated! Everyone has fluid in their head. This fluid has various functions, including stopping the brain from getting dry, feeding the brain with certain nutrients and removing waste products from the brain. Also the fluid acts as a shock absorber to prevent the brain from being shaken too much. However, this fluid must remain in a balanced form in the brain: not too much fluid, and not too little. There is a constant circulation of this fluid around the brain; it comes into the brain and then leaves the brain by being absorbed into the blood vessels.

What Happens to Make the Head So Big?

Most hydrocephalus or "big head" happens in babies, although young adults can get it too. As we have said, the fluid should circulate inside the head. Sometimes there is an obstruction and the fluid cannot drain out of the brain normally, but it still comes into the brain. This problem might be caused by an inability of blood vessels to absorb fluids or by the excessive production of fluids in the brain. The excessive amount of fluid puts too much pressure on the brain, and this pressure causes swelling of the head.

Generally, hydrocephalus happens before birth, while the baby is still in the womb, but it is normally recognized during or after birth. Perhaps the baby had some bleeding on the brain while in the womb, or the mother was ill with an infection. It can also happen later in life as a consequence of a severe head injury or an infection like meningitis. But in many cases, we do not know why it happens.

The important point to understand is this:

Hydrocephalus is not an evil spirit; the child is not bewitched; it is not a punishment. It is simply that there is nowhere for the extra fluid to go, so the head becomes big.

How Can You Recognize a Child with Hydrocephalus?

It is quite easy to recognize a child with hydrocephalus because the child will have an abnormally large head, especially on either side above the ears and over the forehead.

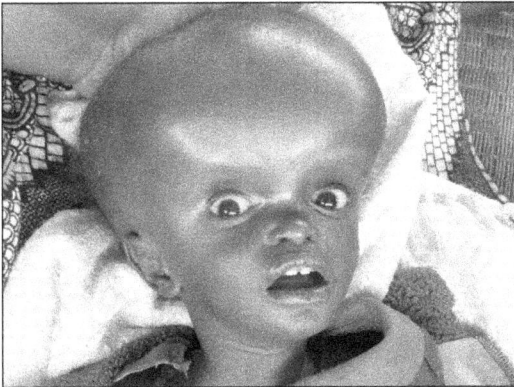

Figure 2.6. A young child with hydrocephalus.
Photo ©Bridget Hathaway.

The head increases in size quite rapidly. The fluid can be felt between the "joints" of the skull: from the forehead backwards to the back of the skull. The eyes look like a setting sun – that is, the pupils of the eyes are low down. The child may have epileptic fits, vomit a lot, feel sleepy, be unable to walk or balance, or suffer severe headaches. They may have vision problems.

What Is the Treatment for Hydrocephalus?

The child with a big head will need to be seen by a specialist doctor, who will probably operate on the child. The doctor will put a tiny plastic tube into the brain that will take the fluid away from the brain into the body, where the fluid will be absorbed naturally. This tube is called a "shunt system."

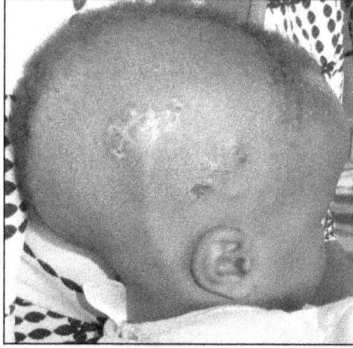

Figure 2.7. A child after surgery to fit a shunt system.
Photo ©Bridget Hathaway.

The tube has a valve that stops the fluid from flowing the wrong way back into the brain. The head will then reduce in size, although this depends on the age at which the child is operated on. It is best to operate at an early age. Do not use local medicine to treat the child; this can cause the child pain and suffering and may lead to burns on the head, as you can see in the picture.

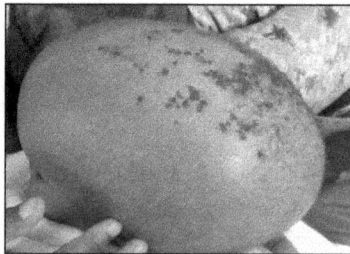

Figure 2.8. Burns on the head as a result of local medicine.
Photo ©Bridget Hathaway.

Cleft Lip and Cleft Palate

What Is a Cleft Lip?

Cleft means "split" or "separation." Therefore a cleft lip is when part of the lip is separated or split.

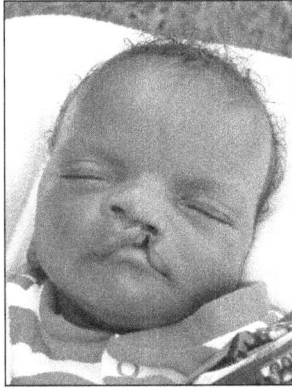

Figure 2.9. Cleft lip in a young baby. Photo ©Bridget Hathaway.

It is a birth defect. During early pregnancy, different areas of the face develop individually and then join together; the lip forms at this stage. If the lip is not formed properly, the result is a cleft or break in the lip. It can be a small division in the coloured part of the lip or a complete break in one or both sides of the lip. The opening appears in the upper lip between the mouth and nose and sometimes extends into the nose. Children with a cleft lip may also have a cleft palate.

What Is a Cleft Palate?

If you put your tongue up to the roof of your mouth, you will feel that it is one complete piece. A cleft palate describes when the roof of the mouth has not joined completely during pregnancy. A cleft palate can vary from just an opening at the back of the mouth to a nearly complete break in the roof of the mouth.

Children with cleft lip and palate encounter several challenges. It is very hard for the baby to breastfeed, and even feeding from a spoon can be difficult. Children with cleft palate experience difficulty with eating and, due to the split in the lip and roof of the mouth, will have speech problems. Children with a cleft lip may be shy, afraid of meeting people and very sad, especially girls, as they cannot hide the deformity on their faces. The family may be very upset, and sometimes a husband will blame his wife and leave her so he can take another wife. Sometimes the family will not look after the child, hoping that he or she will die.

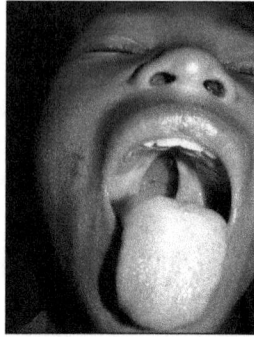

Figure 2.10. The gap in the roof of the mouth; a cleft palate.
Photo ©Bridget Hathaway.

What Causes Cleft Lip and Palate?

We know *what* happens, but we do not know exactly *why* the lip or palate doesn't form properly. It might be something that is inherited from the parents. Just as we inherit the shape of our faces or how tall we will grow, so a baby might inherit a cleft lip and palate. This does not necessarily mean that one of the parents has a cleft lip, but that they have carried it in their genes. Like other disabilities, certain actions during pregnancy may be contributing factors to cleft lip and palate; such actions include smoking and the use of harmful medicines not recommended to pregnant women.

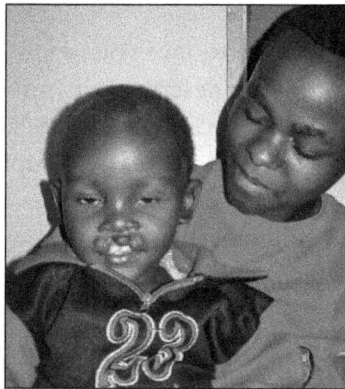

Figure 2.11. Deus before surgery.
Photo ©Bridget Hathaway.

What Is the Treatment for Cleft Lip and Palate?

Cleft lip and palate can be repaired through surgery and the outcome is usually very good.

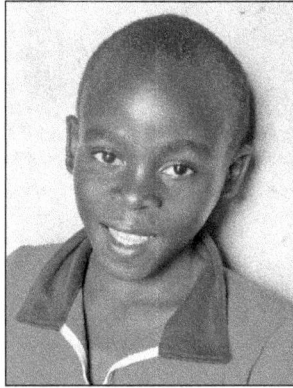

Figure 2.12. Deus a few years after surgery.
Photo ©Bridget Hathaway.

The surgery can be done at any time, but it is important that the repair is done as early as possible, when the child is young, so that his or her language learning is not delayed. Children with cleft lip and palate have no problems in their brains. They can go to school and learn like other children.

Cleft lip and palate is not caused by a sin in the mother's life; or by a child being bewitched; or by the mother having said bad words about someone. It is not anyone's fault.

Club Foot

What Is Club Foot?

Club foot is when one or both feet are turned inwards, which causes a child to walk on the outside of the foot with the sole of the foot turned inward and upward.

Although club foot often occurs in isolation, sometimes it is a complication of spina bifida or cerebral palsy. It is a birth defect which may occur in either one foot or both feet.

What Causes Club Foot?

The cause is unknown, although it is suggested that the foot or feet were positioned that way in the womb. However, while we are not sure why club foot happens, we should understand that it is not caused by a curse or because of an evil spirit.

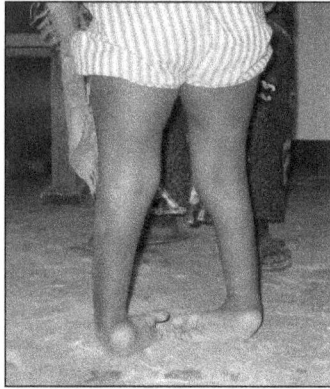

Figure 2.13. An older child with club feet.
Photo ©Bridget Hathaway.

What Is the Treatment for a Child with Club Foot?

A child with club foot should be identified as early as possible and sent for treatment, as in childhood the bones are still soft and flexible and will respond easily. In childhood the treatment of club foot may not cause too much pain, whereas adults will suffer pain and will find their activities affected. Local health facilities or rehabilitation workers can advise parents on the best place to take their child for treatment. When a child starts treatment, the parents should be encouraged to be patient as it will take a long time and will involve several visits to the hospital. It is very important that there is close follow-up of the child to ensure that he or she follows all the instructions and attends all the appointments with a doctor, because there is a danger of the foot returning to its original position; if this happens, it will require another operation, which is harder to do.

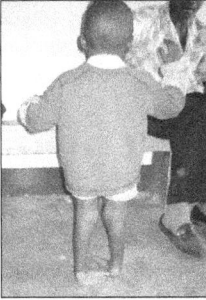

Figures 2.14. Stavius before and after surgery.
Photo ©Bridget Hathaway.

Summary

By explaining about certain disabilities we can bring clarity about the facts of disability, thus removing the misunderstanding surrounding the origin of disabling conditions. When we begin to understand a little more about the body and the way it functions, the fears regarding bodies that are different will subside. When we ourselves have understanding, we can reassure those around us that sin and evil spirits are not the cause of disability, thus opening the way for all people to be welcomed into the Christian family – both those who are able-bodied and those who have a disability.

3

Intellectual Impairment

Let us begin with questions that you might ask when you meet with a child or adult with an intellectual impairment: "Ibrahim's behaviour is very strange. Do you think he has a bad spirit in him? Why does he laugh like that and do unexpected things?"

Intellectual impairment is often the least understood of all disabilities, and children who have problems learning like others may suffer from neglect and abusive treatment. What is the reason behind this? Perhaps it is because we expect certain responses and codes of behaviour from our fellow human beings. For example, if someone says to you, "My mother is very ill in hospital – she might die," your normal response would be to give sympathy and say how sorry you are. Someone with intellectual impairment might not understand the words spoken, or the seriousness of the situation; that person might even laugh because they are happy to see you. You might then interpret this by thinking that the person has a bad spirit and is laughing at misfortune. This is an example of how a lack of understanding causes a wrong response. It is important to remember that throughout this chapter.

What Are the Causes of Intellectual Impairment?

There is no quick answer to this question, so here we outline some of the possible causes of intellectual impairment.

Often, it is part of a complex mix of disabilities; for example, in moderate and severe spastic cerebral palsy there may be a mix of physical and intellectual impairments together with epilepsy. Cerebral palsy is often a result of a difficult birth, when the newborn baby lacked oxygen, causing brain damage.

Sometimes, children are entirely normal apart from a difficulty in learning the same way as others of their age. Their impairment may be caused by an illness of their mothers during pregnancy, such as rubella, or by their mothers having taken local medicine that is harmful to use during pregnancy.

The development of the foetus can be harmed during pregnancy by excessive use of alcohol and use of illegal drugs such as marijuana.

Certain types of intellectual impairment are genetic in origin. For example, Down's syndrome is a genetic condition that results in some level of intellectual impairment and a particular range of physical characteristics. These characteristics are present to a greater or lesser extent in all children with Down's syndrome.

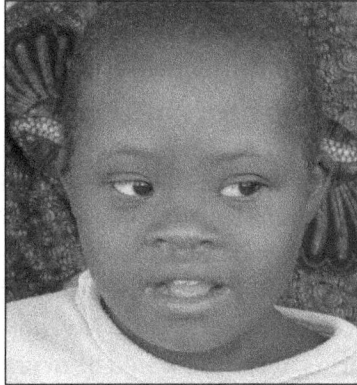

Figure 3.1. A schoolchild with Down's Syndrome.
Photo ©Bridget Hathaway.

Often, the children will have eyes that slant slightly upwards, may have thicker necks than other children and may be shorter in stature. There may be some speech and hearing impairment. People with Down's syndrome are usually very sociable, enjoying making friendships and showing their affection with hugs.

Down's syndrome is caused by the presence of an extra piece of genetic material that is not normally present in other children. *This is not the fault of the mother or the father; it just occurs occasionally at the conception of the baby.*

Autism

Another type of intellectual impairment is known as autism. However, autism is difficult to categorize as some people with autism have high intelligence, while others find the normal learning process very confusing. The common feature in autism is behavioural differences from most people in society. Another key feature in autism is difficulty making relationships, along with hypersensitivity to sound and colour.

Sometimes people with autism behave in ways that cause people to say, "They are possessed by a demon." But their behaviour does not mean they are possessed by a demon; the truth is that a person with autism sees the world in a different way from many of us. Maybe we should ask: Can we truly be the judge of whether a person is demon possessed if we don't understand the causes of impairments? Sometimes children with autism have severe problems in communicating verbally, but they are very intelligent. Are we going to beat the demon out of such a child, who only sees the world in a different way from us? Is God pleased with such actions? In Matthew 18, when Jesus was asked about greatness, this is how he responded: "He called a little child to him, and placed the child among them. And he said: 'Truly I tell you, unless you change and become like little children, you will never enter the kingdom of heaven. Therefore, whoever takes the lowly position of this child is the greatest in the kingdom of heaven. And whoever welcomes one such child in my name welcomes me'" (Matt 18:2–5).

Developmental Delay

Some children have developmental delay; there are a variety of causes of this condition. Although there can be a genetic element or the presence of a rare syndrome, it is more frequently the result of a poor environment with inadequate nutrition or even malnutrition during the early years of development.

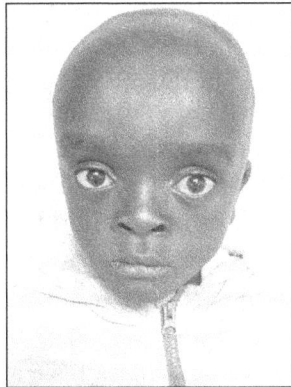

Figure 3.2. This child has genetically inherited intellectual impairment.
Photo ©Bridget Hathaway.

A developing brain needs a good balanced diet in order for the cells to grow and mature. Constant poor nutrition together with a serious lack of stimulation in the home environment can result in permanent brain damage.

Although we have given various causes of intellectual impairment, in many cases we do not know the cause. This can seem difficult to accept, but the gift of a child just as they are, is a gift God asks us to accept.

The Vulnerability of People with Intellectual Impairment

Children and young people with intellectual impairment are often very vulnerable to abuse. Often, they are very trusting of adults and may not have the insight to understand that others may have harmful motives in their relationships with them. Sadly, rape and sexual abuse of girls and young women who have intellectual impairment takes place far too often, resulting in pregnancies that the young women may find hard to handle and babies that they struggle to care for. In many cases, these babies are cared for by family members. Sometimes rape takes place because of local beliefs concerning sexual activity with disabled women. This is explained in chapter 6. Young women with Down's syndrome often enjoy the attention of male friends and are able to flirt with men without realizing the consequences. It is of the utmost importance to teach these young women how to remain safe, such as how to dress nicely without inviting wrong attention, what is good and bad touch, and how to refuse unexpected offers of lifts in cars or on motorbikes. If a family has a young woman who has limited understanding it is often helpful for them to speak with a doctor or the family planning clinic to receive advice on how to keep her safe.

Boys and young men can also be subject to abuse, but not necessarily of a sexual nature. They may be given hard manual work for which they are promised pay, but then they are not paid or are only given food as payment. Malachi 3:5 says, "'So I will come to put you on trial. I will be quick to testify against sorcerers, adulterers and perjurers, against those who defraud labourers of their wages, who oppress the widows and the fatherless, and deprive the foreigners among you of justice, but do not fear me,' says the Lord Almighty." People with disability have as much right to a fair wage for their work as anyone else, as we read in that text.

Children with intellectual impairment have a right to education like all other children, as agreed in the UN Convention on the Rights of the Child

Articles 23, 28 and 29.[1] Only one UN member state has not ratified the signing of the convention, this being the USA.[2] Conventional schooling may not be appropriate for some children, but most children with intellectual impairment will benefit greatly from inclusion either in mainstream education or in a special school catering for their particular needs. If you as pastors can advocate on behalf of these children and their families regarding education, it could open the door for the children to develop enough skills to gain some employment as they grow older. Young people with intellectual impairment can learn skills that are useful in simple employment, such as vegetable preparation in a restaurant, house cleaning, looking after goats and craft skills. We should look for positive opportunities for these young people, rather than continually cry, "They cannot be employed."

Summary

God created each person in his own image. We read this in Genesis 1:26–27. You may think that people with intellectual impairment cannot be made in God's image; we look at this in more detail in chapter 8. People with intellectual impairment often have their own ways of experiencing Christ; there is great joy in seeing a young person with intellectual impairment praising God with no doubts in his or her mind that Jesus is the Son of God. Such people might not understand to the same intellectual depths that we do, but God speaks to their spirits; he knows them and understands them. We should accept them in our church family too.

1. UN Convention on the Rights of the Child, 2 September 1990, accessed 20 August 2018, https://www.ohchr.org/en/professionalinterest/pages/crc.aspx.

2. "How We Protect Children's Rights," UNICEF, accessed 19 December 2018, https://www.unicef.org.uk/what-we-do/un-convention-child-rights/.

4

Sensory Impairment

Sensory impairment affects the functions of human senses: hearing, sight, smell, touch and taste. People usually gather information from the world through hearing and seeing; therefore, if one of the organs responsible for collecting and interpreting information is affected, the interaction of the individual with the surrounding world will decrease. In this chapter we look at visual and hearing impairments as major types of sensory disability.

What Is Visual Impairment?

The term "visual impairment" encompasses all degrees of vision loss. It might be mild or severe, even total blindness. Visual impairment can be classified into two main categories: blindness and low vision. The term "blindness" might mean seeing nothing at all; however, in some cases there may be some perception of light and dark. Some people may have a little vision but not useful vision. This means they might see an outline of an object but cannot identify it.

Many eye specialists agree that the term "low vision" means a permanent reduction of vision that cannot be corrected by medical intervention or spectacles, although these may improve the eyesight slightly. Often this means that everyday tasks are hard or impossible to do without assistance.

How to Identify a Person with Visual Impairment

Visual impairment should be identified as early as possible in order for the family to receive help in adjusting to the situation. Early identification is possible if the parents are attentive to their child's development. Have you ever wondered why a child doesn't do things like other children? For example, at three months of age, if children are unable to follow a coloured object or light moving in front of them, or if they delay in using their hands, or don't move around like other children, or often bump into things, this may be an indication of a sight problem. If children cannot read words on the blackboard or cannot read small print in a book when they begin school, it might indicate vision problems. If you observe some of the above signs in a person, please refer them to the eye department of a hospital.

What Are the Causes of Blindness and Low Vision?

There are many causes of blindness and low vision, but here we will describe just a few. Before discussing the causes, it is important to be aware that visual impairment can occur at any time in life. Diseases such as measles and sexually transmitted diseases (STDs) may affect the organs responsible for sight. If a pregnant woman suffers from these diseases, she may give birth to a child with visual impairment. Eye diseases such as glaucoma and cataracts cause visual impairment too, and are most common in older people.

Figure 4.1. Testing the eyesight of an older person at a village clinic.
Photo ©Bridget Hathaway.

People who are diabetic are at high risk of acquiring sight problems. Injuries caused by sharp objects penetrating the eye are another cause of visual impairment. The use of local medicine for eye treatment is extremely dangerous and can cause blindness. Malnutrition in pregnant women can affect the development of the foetus and can cause visual impairment to the unborn baby. A lack of vitamin A in the diet can cause "night blindness" in which a person cannot see at night. Vitamin A is present in yellow- and orange-coloured fruit and vegetables, such as carrots, papaya and mangoes. There are also some cases of hereditary visual impairments, but this is not common.

Challenges Faced in Visual Impairment and How to Minimize Them

People with visual impairment face many challenges at a social, economic and environmental level. For example, a person who is blind may find it difficult to participate in some activities, such as sports and social events. If society is not aware of visual impairment, people with this type of disability might be denied their rights, including rights to education, marriage and having families, and inheritance. Mobility is another challenge to people with visual impairment; it is difficult in a rural African environment where the ground is often uneven, but also in a town where there are many vehicles and hazards. Those with visual impairments should familiarize themselves with the environment surrounding them, and practise using any equipment in the house or compound. It is very important to leave walkways clear and to keep all equipment in one location, to prevent injuries.

When you meet a person with visual impairment, positive communication is very important; for example, make sure you introduce yourself and everyone else who is present. When guiding a person with visual impairment, give clear explanations and descriptions of where you are, where you are going together and any obstacles in the path. Never leave blind people in a free space; at least locate them near a wall or door. When you identify those with visual impairment who have not received advice, encourage them to see an eye specialist for investigation and appropriate support. Always discourage the use of local medicines in the eyes, as they can seriously damage the eyes and lead to blindness.

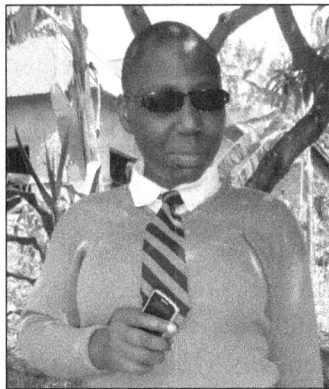

Figure 4.2. Elieth studies at secondary school. She lost her sight through the use of local medicine. Photo ©Bridget Hathaway.

Visual impairment does not affect the intellectual capacity of an individual; therefore, encourage parents to take their children who are visually impaired to school, or advocate on their behalf with the local education department for their right to specialist schooling.

Hearing Impairment

Hearing impairment covers various levels of hearing loss, from mild to profound. This means that a person with hearing impairment might hear nothing at all, or only partially. People with hearing impairment may have some difficulty in understanding and interpreting speech; some may need a hearing aid to improve their hearing capacity, while others may not hear at all even if they use a hearing aid. People who can hear nothing are considered to be deaf. People who are born deaf will also have problems speaking because they have never heard speech. People who lose their hearing after acquiring spoken language may be able to communicate by speech, but with limitations. However, this will depend on the severity or level of hearing loss, and they may not deliver clear speech. Sometimes they have problems controlling the pitch of their voice. In some cases of hearing loss, people have difficulty hearing when there is excessive noise around them.

What Are the Causes of Hearing Impairment?

Hearing impairment, like other impairments or disability conditions, may occur before, during or after birth. Genetic abnormalities in the ear may affect proper development of parts of the ear that support hearing. Injuries to the ear or the head may damage the ear itself, the brain or nerves responsible for hearing. Other injuries might occur at birth if the delivery of the baby is difficult or takes place in an unsafe environment. Some babies are born with hearing impairment due to infections or illnesses that the mother had while she was pregnant and which may have affected the development of the inner ear. It is very important that pregnant women get good nutrition as this contributes to the development of the foetus; poor nutrition may hinder the development of the unborn baby. Premature babies are at high risk of hearing impairment as their organs are immature and easily damaged. Some infections and illnesses, if they are not treated well, can lead to hearing impairment; measles, chicken pox and meningitis are examples of these. Chronic ear infections may damage the structure of the inner ear and cause hearing loss. Some medications and local herbs may be harmful to the ear; it is therefore recommended that you seek a doctor's advice before applying any medication for hearing problems. As we grow old, each part of our bodies grows old too; therefore, old age increases the risk of becoming hearing-impaired. Excessive noise, whether it happens suddenly or persists for a long time, may cause permanent damage to the inner ear; for example, playing loud music through headphones.

Is It Easy to Recognize a Person with Hearing Impairment?

It is quite difficult to recognize hearing impairment in babies because they have not yet developed communication skills. But parents begin realizing there may be a problem when the baby is not responding to sounds or voices, and acquirement of speech is delayed. As the child grows up, you will notice that they are not responding to instructions or give wrong responses to them. People with hearing impairment often ask you to repeat what you have said or will look carefully at your face when you are speaking.

Can People with Hearing Impairment Enjoy Life Like Other People?

People with hearing impairment can live normal lives and even achieve more than other people. It sometimes seems as if God has compensated them for their impairment by giving them another skill. People with hearing impairment are often gifted in art, and they can participate fully in social life if given the opportunity. It is important to ensure that children with hearing impairment are taken to school like other children; however, it is best if they attend a special school for the deaf where they will learn sign language and lip reading, and can socialize with other children. This form of communication might be a challenge in the society where a person with hearing impairment lives, but deaf people try as hard as possible to ensure that others understand what they are trying to communicate. Sometimes they use writing to communicate, especially if they went to school. When you communicate with a person with hearing impairment, make sure you speak clearly and not too fast, and ensure that the environment has no disrupting noises. Make sure you draw the person's attention and that they can see your face. Try to use simple and clear words, and, if the person does not understand, repeat what you have said. In public communications, it is important to have an interpreter in sign language who can facilitate communication.

People with hearing impairment need to take special care when walking along roads because they cannot hear the traffic. They should always walk facing the traffic and look carefully before crossing the road.

Encourage a person with hearing problems to visit a hospital for testing and appropriate treatment. A person with hearing loss can benefit from a hearing aid to boost his or her hearing capacity, but these are not always appropriate in rural areas, where replacement batteries are unlikely to be available and health facilities holding a store of batteries may be far away. Remember to counsel people to seek help in prevention and proper treatment of diseases and infections from health professionals rather than using local medicine.

Summary

People with sensory impairment can take an active part in the church and hold positions of responsibility. For example, people with visual impairment are often good musicians, playing the keyboard, drums or guitar, or they can become members of the choir. They can learn the words and music of songs by listening to them. Those with hearing impairment can be members of the church welcoming team. People with sensory impairment can get married, have families and live family lives like anyone else. They have the same rights to education, health care and inheritance as others in society. As pastors, you can make a difference to society's attitudes by supporting people with sensory impairment, advocating on their behalf and including them in your church family.

5

Other Types of Disability

It is possible you are asking a question like this: "What do you mean by 'other types of disability'? Surely every disability is physical, intellectual or sensory?"

Whenever we try to categorize things to do with human beings, we usually find there are exceptions, because each person is a unique creation. Likewise, disabilities do not fit neatly into categories. In this chapter we will look at four types of disability that do not fit well into the categories of physical, intellectual or sensory disability.

Sickle-Cell Anaemia (SCA)

We will begin by looking at sickle-cell anaemia. Although some people may call this an illness, living with sickle-cell anaemia can limit a person from active participation in certain activities and it is a lifelong condition for which there is no cure. In this respect we can put sickle-cell anaemia in the category of disability.

Sickle-cell anaemia affects the blood cells in the person's body. It is a genetic condition that passes from both parents to the baby. It is not the fault of either parent, and it is not infectious; you cannot catch it from someone who has it. It is a lifelong disorder and at present there is no cure for it through medicine, but people with sickle-cell anaemia can live like other people, with a few limitations, if they look after their health. The parents may not have the condition themselves, but if they both carry the faulty gene, there is a 1 in 4 possibility that one of their children will be born with the condition.[1]

---

1. "Overview: Sickle Cell Disease," NHS, accessed 22 August 2018, https://www.nhs.uk/conditions/sickle-cell-disease/.

The Difference between Normal Blood Cells and Sickle Blood Cells

The blood cells in our body contain haemoglobin, which is what gives the blood its red colour. The haemoglobin in the blood cells carries oxygen round the body, so the blood cells are vital for good health. The blood cells are round in shape, but in someone with sickle-cell disease many of the blood cells are sickle-shaped. Normal blood cells carry enough oxygen to keep the body well supplied and they flow through the blood vessels easily because they are round. Sickle-shaped cells cannot carry so much oxygen because of their shape, they have a shorter lifespan than normal cells and they can become stuck in the blood vessels because of their shape. When they get stuck, it is called a "sickle-cell crisis" and it causes severe pain; the person may be hospitalized. The short lifespan of the cells means the person is at risk of becoming anaemic; if this becomes severe the person may need a blood transfusion. There are other symptoms which need careful treatment; therefore those with SCA should never delay seeing a doctor if they feel unwell. Women with SCA can become pregnant but they should always give birth at hospital in case of complications.

Management of Sickle-Cell Anaemia

It is important that people with sickle-cell disease eat a healthy diet with plenty of fruit and green vegetables, especially spinach or any dark green vegetables. This will ensure they have plenty of vitamins and iron in their diet, which will boost their immune system and stimulate red blood cell production.

Although an almost normal lifestyle is possible, it is important for children to understand that they should drink plenty of fluids, as dehydration can lead to a sickle-cell crisis. They can play sport, but they may tire quickly and become breathless, so care must be taken as to how much sport they play. A person with SCA can study like anyone else, go to school and university, and enter employment.

People with SCA can take an active part in church activities and be welcomed into the church family.

Psychiatric Disorders

Psychiatric disorders are not the same as learning impairment, although it is often assumed they are the same thing. Someone who has a psychiatric disorder may be very intelligent but has an imbalance in the brain. Equally, someone with a learning impairment often has no psychological distress, but only brain damage. The key difference between psychiatric disorders and learning impairment is that learning impairment is a permanent condition that cannot change through the use of medication, whereas psychiatric disorders may be temporary or lifelong, and can be controlled by the use of medication. In fact, if someone takes medication as advised by the doctor, they may be able to live a normal life.

In many countries, speaking about physical disability is acceptable, but talking about psychological disturbance is something we like to hide. Why is this so? Perhaps it has its roots in our difficulty in accepting and understanding unpredictable or irrational behaviour. We are afraid of what we cannot understand or explain. Our reaction is to label people as "mad" or "possessed" and avoid them; if they come into church, we send them out. But is this what Jesus did?

A Brief Look at Different Psychiatric Conditions

Psychological disturbance, or mental illness as it is more commonly known, is a term that covers many conditions affecting the mind. Most conditions interfere with daily life but are not life-threatening; however, more severe cases of mental illness can be life-threatening. It is not necessary to study each condition in detail in this book, but we will acknowledge some conditions that you may have heard about.

People living with psychosis often cannot distinguish between reality and a fantasy world. They might have hallucinations, hear voices and experience panic and fear. Their condition can be controlled by medication, but often we allow these people to live on the streets, sinking deeper and deeper into their own worlds.

We have all heard of depression. Often people will describe themselves as feeling miserable. This is normal for all of us at certain times, but when "feeling miserable" continues for a long period and affects how we sleep and eat, and gives us poor concentration and extreme tiredness, we might be experiencing depression. It might not be necessary to take tablets; talking over our worries, fears and sadness with someone who can listen well and guide our thoughts in a positive way may be all that is needed. When a person swings from being very excitable and energetic to very depressed and unable to do anything, that person's condition is called manic depression.

Schizophrenia is a condition in which someone may have delusions. For example, a man who sees a policeman walk past may be convinced that the policeman has been sent to arrest him for stealing a cow that was reported missing by a neighbour. The man is convinced he stole the cow. People with schizophrenia may dress strangely and inappropriately, find verbal communication difficult and begin to lose their original personality. Correct medication and community support is of great importance.

For all psychiatric conditions, professional medical help should be sought. Correct medication might even mean the difference between a person living or dying, but in most cases it will enable that person to live actively in the community. However, the use of local medicine might make the condition worse, so it is wise to get a doctor's advice before using it.

If we, as Christians, cannot show Christ's love and understanding to people with psychological disturbance, who will? Did Jesus reject them or accept them? What will you do when you are given a parish and meet people like those we have described?

Albinism

Albino people, or people with albinism, have suffered greatly in many African countries; the extent of their torment should shock us. As pastors, you can make a difference in opposing the damaging beliefs that surround albinism and receive our brothers and sisters into the church family.

Albinism affects people from every country, whether they are normally of a pale skin, like people in Britain or the Netherlands, or of a light brown skin, like people in Asia. It does not matter if you are male or female, rich or poor: albinism can affect the family.

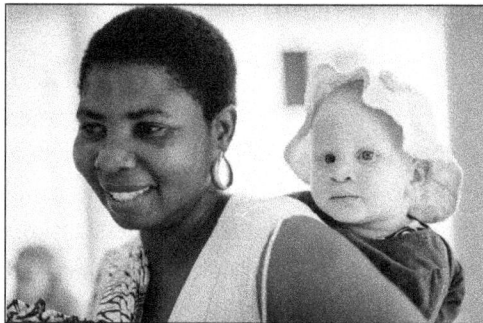

Figure 5.1. A mother with her child with albinism.
Photo ©Chihiro Tagata, Standing Voice. Used by permission.

You probably know of families where both parents have dark skin and the child has albinism. People say of the father, "How can that be his child?

He is black and the child is white." Albinism is a genetic condition, inherited from both parents; both the mother and the father pass it on to the child. The parents may not have albinism themselves but they carry the faulty gene. If you ask the family about grandparents, great-grandparents and even generations much earlier, you may hear of people with albinism in the family.

What Causes Albinism?

Every person has something called pigment, or colouring, in their hair, skin and eyes. The colouring is called *melanin*. If someone has a lot of melanin, that person will have a dark skin and dark hair; black African people have a lot of melanin in their skin, hair and eyes. However, if someone has only a little melanin, he or she will have pale skin and light-coloured hair and eyes. White British people have a smaller amount of melanin in their skin, hair and eyes than black African people. The difference is only the amount of melanin. People who have albinism have only a small amount of melanin, even when they are African, and this means that their skin is pale and their hair is light brown.

Are People with Albinism Special?

People with albinism are human beings like you and I. They desire to be treated with respect and dignity, just like you and I. We can help by accepting them as fellow human beings who just happen to have a different colour skin from us.

- *They have no special powers. Their bones, teeth and fingernails are the same as ours.*
- *If you have AIDS and have sex with a woman who has albinism, it will not cure you of AIDS. All that will happen is that you will give her AIDS.*
- *There is absolutely no magic in a person with albinism. You will not become rich, find gold or catch more fish by using a part of that person's body.*
- *God made some of us with a lot of melanin and some of us with little melanin. But we are all children of God.*

How Can People with Albinism Protect Their Bodies?

When skin is pale it can be affected by the sun, causing skin cancer, which may be terminal. The best advice for people with albinism is to wear long-sleeved shirts and large hats to prevent damage from the sun. Dry skin is also a problem, so daily use of skin lotion is important; if possible, they should use a type that gives protection from the sun.

Figure 5.2. A child with albinism wearing protective clothing.
Photo ©Harry Freeland, Standing Voice. Used by permission.

The lack of pigment in the eyes causes people with albinism to have weak eyesight and be affected by bright light. It is therefore wise to seek the advice of a specialist eye doctor. Wearing sunglasses will protect the eyes and prevent further damage. A person with albinism can marry and have a family; however, if two people with albinism marry, their children are likely to have albinism too.

How Can People with Albinism Protect Their Rights?

As church leaders, we have the opportunity to make a difference for people with albinism. How? We can make a difference by educating the community about albinism and by bringing change in people's harmful beliefs; and by advocating on behalf of people with albinism for better security, improved health care, inclusion in education and acceptance in the community. Organizations working for the rights of people with albinism have useful information and advice for anyone interested in supporting them through advocacy.[2] Let us welcome people with albinism to church and allow them the freedom to be part of our church family.

---

2. See, for example, Under the Same Sun, https://www.underthesamesun.com/; the Josephat Torner Foundation, https://www.jtfe.org/; and the Tanzania Albinism Society, https://www.betterplace.org/en/organisations/10856-tanzania-albinism-society.

Figure 5.3. Educating school children about albinism. Photo ©Ebrahim Mirmalek, Standing Voice. Used by Permission.

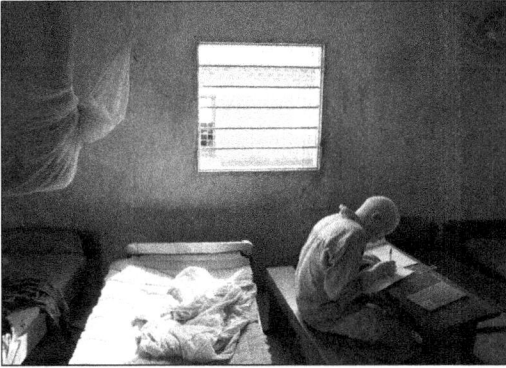

Figure 5.4. A school pupil with albinism studying hard. Photo ©Harry Freeland, Standing Voice. Used by Permission.

Genetic Counselling

As a pastor, you will be involved in marriage preparation classes for couples planning marriage. It is important that couples agree to being tested not only for HIV but also for genetic conditions, if this option is available. If they both carry a faulty gene that might result in a child with disability, they can make an informed choice whether to continue with the marriage, and, if they do so, accept the limitations on having children that this might indicate.

Epilepsy

Why is epilepsy under the heading of "other" disabilities? You might expect it to be under "intellectual impairment," but that indicates a wrong assumption. Most people living with epilepsy have no intellectual impairment at all. Someone who has controlled epilepsy can study at university, be a Member of Parliament or be a teacher. Often we cannot know if someone has epilepsy because he or she seems perfectly "normal" to us. The problem arises when the epilepsy is not treated and the person suffers brain damage from continual seizures.

When we talk about epilepsy, people often say, "Oh, I am afraid of epilepsy!" This is not surprising, because it can be frightening to see someone having an epileptic seizure. The person's actions appear uncontrolled, and it is easy to believe people when they say, "There is a demon in that person!" However, when we understand what is happening when someone has a seizure, our fear subsides because we recognize the cause of the condition. (We will look at beliefs about epilepsy in chapter 6.) In some African traditions there is a belief that seizures take place on a certain date or when the moon is in a specific phase. This is not true; seizures can take place at any time.[3]

What Is Epilepsy?

Epilepsy is a condition of the brain affecting the "electricity" in the brain. Messages are continually travelling from the brain to the body along the nerves, which communicate to each other through "messages" that are like little shots of electricity. These messages are sent constantly for every action that we do. When an epileptic seizure takes place, it is like a short circuit in the electricity in the brain. All the messages rush together and become confused, resulting in the body losing control. There are many different types of epilepsy, but they all result from the "electricity" in the brain breaking down. In this chapter we are looking at one type of epilepsy.

Many people say that epilepsy is infectious, but this is not true. If it were true, the parents and siblings of someone with epilepsy would have the condition too, as would doctors and nurses. Everything that happens occurs inside the brain; there is nothing that can infect you with epilepsy. Even when people with epilepsy dribble saliva or urinate, they cannot infect you with epilepsy.

Looking at the Cause of Epileptic Seizures

Epilepsy can begin at any time of life. Usually there is a reason why it starts, but we cannot always identify the reason. It may begin after a head injury, perhaps from a road accident or falling from a tree. Some serious illnesses such as meningitis, measles, cerebral malaria or a high fever can cause epilepsy; the presence of a brain tumour can trigger a seizure. Long-term use of strong

---

3. "Full Moon 'Does Not Trigger' Seizures," *Epilepsy Today*, 2 June 2004, accessed 20 December 2018, https://www.epilepsy.org.uk/news/full-moon-does-not-trigger-seizures.

alcohol or illegal drugs such as marijuana, cannabis and glue sniffing can also cause epileptic seizures.

Some forms of epilepsy are part of a wider disability diagnosis, such as in spastic cerebral palsy, autism or some uncommon syndromes. It can also occur after a difficult birth in which the baby has suffered some brain damage. Inherited epilepsy is more unusual but can occur.

More Information about Seizures

Seizures can happen in any part of the brain. Some seizures affect both halves of the brain, while others affect only a small part of the brain. The way the person acts during the seizure depends on which part of the brain is affected; however, sometimes more than one part of the brain is involved in a seizure.

Sometimes a person will know beforehand when a seizure is about to happen; the person has what is called an "aura," or a certain feeling. However, some people have no warning of a seizure. There are many types of aura; for example, people with epilepsy might have a strange taste in their mouths or smell something that isn't there. They might complain of a strange feeling in their stomachs, or suddenly become very agitated. It is useful to recognize an aura because then action can be taken before the seizure happens. Find a sheltered safe place nearby where they can sit down; sit them on the floor or ground, not on a chair, and clear a space around them; this prevents injury if the person has a seizure. Stay with them, and when they are conscious again give reassurance that you will stay with them until they feel better. Usually the person will feel very tired after a seizure and will fall asleep for a time.

If you are there when the person has the seizure, the first thing to do is to keep calm! You will not be helpful if you panic. Again, make sure the person is in a safe place, away from fire, a road, water or anything that could be dangerous. Place something soft under the person's head if you can (though this is not essential); it is also useful to loosen any tight clothing, especially round the person's neck. Do not put anything in the person's mouth as this can be dangerous. Lay the person in the recovery position when his or her body has relaxed a little, placing the head to the side so that the tongue will fall forwards, not backwards, which would block the throat.

Treatment for Epilepsy

If people tell you there is no treatment for epilepsy, do not believe them. Epilepsy can be controlled well on most occasions through medication. There are tablets that can help control seizures, or even prevent them occurring. The doctor or specialist nurse at the health centre or hospital can advise on the appropriate medication and dosage for the person concerned. This advice must be followed exactly. Never mix medicine from the pharmacy with local medicine; this can be very dangerous. The local healer is unable to treat epilepsy effectively.

It is *essential* for the person to take the tablets every day without fail, because if they stop taking them, there is a likelihood of seizures returning. The tablets work by controlling the "electricity" in the brain, keeping it in an even pattern. The seizures are controlled or stopped because of the tablets, and only the doctor can advise the person as to when he or she can cease taking the medication. Drinking alcohol when taking the medication will severely reduce its effectiveness.

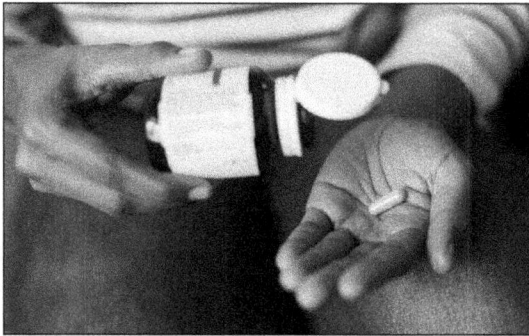

Figure 5.5. Daily medication is essential in most cases of epilepsy.
Photo ©Rawpixel.com - stock.adobe.com.

People with epilepsy can live normal lives; however, there are certain activities they should avoid. It is not advised that they climb trees or ladders. Cooking alone by an open fire is dangerous; even an adult with epilepsy should have someone nearby in case of a seizure. Children with epilepsy should never be left alone by an open fire. It is advisable to have someone with them when they are collecting water from any water point, and advice should be sought from a doctor before they drive a car or motorbike, or use machinery such as a chain saw.

Be Positive about Epilepsy

Epilepsy is something that people learn to live with. Let them live as normally as possible! The problem often comes from the attitude of society which marginalizes people with epilepsy and their families, denying their natural rights to education and their freedom to work, to worship and to be part of a community. As a pastor who now understands about epilepsy, you can help change the attitude of society towards people with epilepsy.

Summary

Three of the conditions we have talked about in this chapter – albinism, mental health conditions, and epilepsy – are frequently the object of intense discrimination. It is hoped that, as church workers, we can play a part in reducing the stigma that people so often suffer when diagnosed with these conditions, and that we can be an example for other people to follow.

6

Some African Attitudes and Beliefs about Disability

Perhaps you are asking the question, "Why is it necessary for us to look at local beliefs about disability? We are working within our churches; we know the beliefs are not really true."

Beliefs handed down through generations are not easily forgotten or left behind. You might think they are no longer a part of your life, but when you meet a child with a severe disability – for example, a cleft lip – is there a seed of thought in your mind that wonders whether this is a consequence of wrongdoing in the family? Maybe the mother spoke against another person, injuring that person's reputation, and this is God's judgment? Such beliefs can cause immense harm, not just to the person with disability, but also to the family. In addition, society suffers because it loses the contributions of entire families because they are marginalized and disempowered.

The Rain Storm

The following short story shows us how harmful these beliefs can be.

It was the rainy season, and this year the rains were particularly heavy. Mama Sebastien was tired of the rain, and tired of being pregnant. This was her fifth child, and trying to make a living in the suburb of the large town was very hard. Renting a small house was expensive, so they could only afford one near the river, where the prices were cheaper due to the risk of flooding. She sat down, looking at the river racing past and rising fast. As she watched, she began to feel labour pains; she knew the time had come. Calling a neighbour to watch the children, she packed a bag and slowly and painfully struggled in the rain to the health centre. The labour was hard and she was exhausted. "Push harder, Mama Sebastien," the midwife urged, but she had no strength.

At last the baby was born, but there was no cry. The midwife quickly smacked the baby's back and cleared the mouth, but it took some time before a weak cry was heard. Later that day, Mama Sebastien returned home, carrying her newborn baby, who seemed very weak and lifeless. The rain was easing and the sun appearing.

As the baby grew, it became obvious to everyone that there was something seriously wrong. The baby's arms and legs were twisting and moving very strangely. A neighbour visited and commented, "Mama Sebastien, do you remember how, before you gave birth, the river was running high and the rain was terrible, and when the baby was born the rain stopped? Don't you think this child is from the river serpent, that spirit living in the river? Look at the way she moves. You must have upset the spirit. What will you do with her?" The neighbour left the house and began to spread the news. Mama Sebastien wept.

The River Serpent

In chapter 2 we looked at different types of physical disability, so perhaps you are able to identify the condition that Mama Sebastien's baby had. In the story, Mama Sebastien was tired and the birth difficult. The baby was born with cerebral palsy (CP), the type called athetoid (see chapter 2). In this type of CP the movements of the limbs are often uncontrolled, moving in all directions, and it can affect the face too, with strange movements of the mouth and head. In some parts of West Africa it is thought that a baby with this disability is a child from the river serpent, perhaps as a punishment. There is some belief that the child should be returned to the river. The neighbour visiting Mama Sebastien clearly followed the local belief and wanted to spread the news around the local community. How would you feel if this was your child? The probability is that, once the neighbourhood heard this, they would avoid the family, offering advice that would be heard at the market and in the shops: return the child to the river. As a church leader, how would you react when you heard this advice in local gossip? How would you advise Mama Sebastien? How would you handle people who brought this kind of belief to church?

The Snake

The following story tells of something we witnessed in East Africa. During a village clinic for children with disability, a mother brought her young daughter, who was about three years old. The child was unable to walk and had intellectual impairment; she moved by pulling herself along the ground on her stomach. The mother had not taken the child to the local hospital or sought advice to help her with the child. We began working with the girl and eventually, after months of visits, we managed to get her to stand with support, and then to walk using a walking trolley. Throughout this time the mother appeared disengaged, not really convinced we would achieve anything. Eventually, she was ready to tell us the reason for this. Apparently, when she was pregnant with her daughter, she was walking on a village path through the grass when a snake passed right in front of her. She was not bitten, but she was convinced that this meant her child would always move on her belly, like a snake. What was the point in teaching the child to walk? It could never be achieved because of the snake she had seen. Although her daughter could not walk independently, she walked around pushing her trolley. Her mother, pleased at the progress, asked, "Why have you bothered to spend all this time with my child?" This gave us an opportunity to share the meaning of God's love and care for all of his creation, whether disabled or able-bodied. If we had not persevered, the local belief would have left the child on her belly, at great risk of infection, wounds and accidents.

Our Enemy, the Snake

Many people see snakes as their enemy. Perhaps this originates from the story of the fall. In East Africa there are a number of beliefs related to pythons; for example:

- If a pregnant woman sees a python's nest, she must throw a stone into it; this will prevent her baby being born with disability.
- In order to prevent a young child from being harmed, the mother might hang a piece of dry python bone round the child's waist, especially if she saw a snake during her pregnancy.
- If a child is born with athetoid cerebral palsy (like the child in the story), local people will say that, without her knowing, a python must have passed the mother when she was pregnant, and that is why the child moves like a snake.
- If a child has a disability, the mother must take grass from near where a python has been eating grass. She is to take the grass home, pound it and make a medicine from it. The medicine will be used as an enema, and this is believed to heal the disability or prevent disability.

Many of these beliefs are dying out as current generations have access to information from the Internet and television. However, even when a person denies having any such belief, there often remains a seed of it in the background. These beliefs grip people in fear and superstition, in contrast to the freedom Christ gives us through his victory over evil.

Beliefs with a Moral Basis

Laughter is a good thing; it brings happiness when people laugh together. It can also bring healing in relationships. However, not all laughter is gentle; sometimes it is unkind and harmful. We call this *laughter at* or *against* people.

There is a belief that if you give birth to a child with a disability, it is because you have laughed at a person with disability; you mocked that person. The disability in the person you mocked has therefore been given to your child. Do we believe this could be true? Or do we see it as a punishment from God?

Some beliefs have a moral root. It is possible that this local belief arose from the desire to stop the community being unkind to people with disability; by creating a fear of punishment, the elders were preventing negative behaviour towards certain members of society.

If we, as Christians, believe that we are created in God's image and are part of God's family, we will see God in the other person, whether that person is able-bodied or has a disability. We might laugh *with* that person, but not *at* that person.

Beliefs Containing Some Truth

Sometimes a belief has a seed of truth in it; there is a reason why the elders in the past believed certain things and taught them to the following generations. In the past, cultures were largely of an oral tradition, with teaching taking place through stories and fables. Some of the teaching was based on Bible stories mixed with traditional beliefs, and some of those beliefs have persisted down to today even though the source of the belief may have been lost.

One belief is that if a boy has a sexual relationship with his sister, the resulting child will have a disability. There is some scientific truth in this belief. If someone marries a blood relative or has a sexual relationship with a blood relative, the resulting child will inherit from a reduced gene pool. What does this mean? Every baby inherits genes from each parent; if the parents are closely related and have inherited their genes from the same parents or close relatives, any weakness in the genes will become more significant as the generations continue. This is probably why one of the reasons why God frowns on sexual relations within the blood family (Deut 27:20–23). But we must never assume that someone with a disability is the consequence of any action like this; it is very rare, and we should not judge people in this way.

Beliefs Connected with Epilepsy

In African countries, people have various perceptions or beliefs regarding epilepsy. When someone has a seizure it is thought that he or she is caught up by an evil spirit. Epilepsy has been connected with supernatural causes and witchcraft for centuries, including curses and retribution for past deeds. Due to these beliefs, people who have epilepsy have been denied appropriate medical treatment because it is thought that the problem cannot be treated in the hospital but requires traditional healers. This causes the condition to worsen, resulting in intellectual impairment because of repeated seizures. There is some anecdotal evidence that traditional medicine can work, but scientific proof is lacking;[1] frequently, traditional medicine lacks specific dosage, which can lead to overdosing.

The existence of evil spirits cannot be denied, but the presence of epilepsy does not necessarily mean that the person has an evil spirit; in fact, in most cases the person does not have an evil spirit. It is advisable always to think of epilepsy first rather than an evil spirit; only after discernment by an experienced pastor should any intervention other than medication take place. Intervention should never damage the person or his or her family, whether physically, spiritually or emotionally. That is not honouring to God.

There is a belief that if a person with epilepsy falls into fire or water, that person cannot be cured. There is no basis to this belief; it is simply a tradition that has been inherited from previous generations. Indeed, it is mentioned in the account of the epileptic boy in Matthew 17:14–15, but Jesus healed the boy. A person with epilepsy can be treated, even if he or she falls into water or fire; anti-convulsion medication is available at most health centres and, with treatment, there is a good chance the person will live a full life.

There is much discrimination against people with epilepsy and their families. People with epilepsy are not included in social activities and even family events; they often have no opportunity to attend church services because

---

1. Wei Liu et al., "The Effects of Herbal Medicine on Epilepsy," *Oncotarget* 8, no. 29 (18 July 2017): 48385–48397, accessed 24 August 2018, https://www.ncbi.nlm.nih.gov/pmc/articles/PMC5564656/ .

of the mistaken belief that epilepsy is contagious, even from the saliva and urine of a person with epilepsy. This false belief limits the access people with epilepsy have to suitable care, especially during a seizure.

Beliefs Connected with Albinism

Over many generations, African traditional beliefs about albinism have resulted in them being the target of killings and inhumane attacks. People believe that possessing albino body parts will bring them success and wealth; for example, some believe that using albino body parts together with witchcraft practices will help fishermen to catch more fish. Body parts have also been used in mining areas in the belief that they will attract more minerals. Surprisingly, even politicians are believed to have been involved in such things, believing that albino body parts contain magical powers which can increase their popularity. These beliefs have put the lives of people with albinism in great danger; but where can they hide to protect themselves?

In East Africa, people with albinism are sometimes believed to be spirits or ghosts. If they were to disappear, they would be understood to be "just visiting another place." This means that they are in great danger: a child or adult could be killed and their disappearance wouldn't be reported because "they are just ghosts."

In some tribal groups, it is believed that if a brother marries his sister, or a son has sexual relations with his mother, the resulting child will have albinism. This belief persists. This kind of belief severely marginalizes not only the person with albinism, but that person's family too, as they will be looked on with disgust.

But what is the truth? Do we gain success in life only through such practices as have been described here? Of course not! We see many people who have succeeded in their lives; do we believe that they have been involved in these practices? Are they killers of people with albinism? And have you ever asked yourself why the families of people with albinism are not wealthy? Do developed countries have the same belief? These questions should challenge us to think more deeply about our fellow brothers and sisters. There is nothing special in people with albinism; they are just like other people. In order to dispel these myths, joint efforts are needed from community leaders and church leaders to spread correct information to the community about albinism. Church leaders are in a good position to create awareness as they are trusted more than other people in the community.

A Damaged Mouth

In chapter 2 we looked at the conditions of cleft lip and palate; seeing someone with this condition can be a shock, giving rise to the thought, "Why has this happened? What has caused it?" For some reason, disability in other parts of the body is more acceptable than disability on the face, which cannot be hidden.

There are many different beliefs about the cause of cleft lip and palate. In one, it is believed that the mother must have spoken malicious words about someone in the locality, spreading gossip that damaged a person's character. Do you think this could be true? Does God really punish in this way? We hope that through understanding the possible causes of cleft lip, a church member who has a child with cleft lip will not be the subject of such a belief.

A different belief about the origin of cleft lip, again from East Africa, is that during her pregnancy a woman jumped over a vessel used for making local alcohol. This vessel is often made from a tree trunk cut in half lengthwise and hollowed out, inside which the alcohol is brewed.

A further belief comes from East Africa. In the past, women in some tribal traditions were not permitted to eat eggs. If a woman gave birth to a child with a cleft lip, she would be accused of having eaten eggs and broken the tribal tradition. A related common belief is that if a pregnant woman eats eggs, her baby will be born bald, without hair.

Double Trouble

There are many beliefs connected with the birth of twins. In some cultures, twins are a blessing and hold special powers, while in others, to have twins is a scourge. There is a belief that having twins in the family will cause someone in the extended family to have mental health problems. Sometimes, much wealth is lost to witchdoctors in the hope of calming angry spirits, especially if one twin is disabled. However, we will not look further at beliefs about twins, as the focus in this book remains on beliefs and disability.

Plastic Teeth

Do you believe that "plastic teeth" exist in young babies? And do you realize how dangerous this belief is? This is a common belief in some African countries, but what is it exactly that people believe? When her baby suffers from diarrhoea, vomiting or fever, the mother checks the baby and, when looking in the mouth, sees little hard white lumps appearing in the gums.

She thinks the baby has plastic teeth and believes the baby will die unless the teeth are removed. But if you notice carefully, "plastic teeth" appear at the time when a child is approaching the age of developing his or her first teeth; these symptoms are just part of the changes that are happening in the child's body. You may be surprised that even educated people take their children to traditional healers to remove "plastic teeth." Sadly, the children suffer immense pain, lose a lot of blood, get serious infection and may even die. This belief has been passed through generations and continues today. It is a heart-breaking experience to be asked to help a young couple by collecting their baby's body from the hospital and transport it home for burial. What was the cause of death? Massive bleeding and infection caused by a local "healer" trying to remove the supposed "plastic tooth."

What can you do as a church leader if you find that someone is convinced by other people to take his or her child to the traditional healer to remove "plastic teeth"? Please explain to the parents that what they are seeing is a real tooth. If the parents are still worried, advise them to take the child to the health facility. We need to work together to prevent the many deaths that take place annually as a result of this mistaken belief.

Local Beliefs Regarding Intellectual Impairment

In parts of East Africa there is a belief that if a family member has mental health problems and runs into the bush and never returns, subsequent births in that family will produce children with intellectual impairment.

We believe that every child born to a Christian family should be brought to the church for baptism or dedication. How many children with intellectual impairment have been baptized or dedicated in the church you come from? Sometimes it is difficult to know this, but as pastors and evangelists we have an opportunity to welcome all God's children into his church.

Safety for Young Women Who Live with Disability

Did you know that young women with disability are being targeted for rape? It is believed in some places that if a man has sexual relations with a young woman with disability, he will become rich. Young women, many with intellectual impairment, are taken advantage of when their guardians are away from home, perhaps at work, or when they are collecting water or firewood. The attack is not only traumatic for the woman but often results in an unwanted pregnancy;

and with no witnesses, it can be difficult to bring a court case. Sometimes the pregnancy endangers the life of the young woman.

Pastors and evangelists may well have the opportunity to challenge this harmful belief. Jesus's example was very different: he cared for the outcast and respected the marginalized, as we read in the parable of the sheep and the goats in Matthew 25:31–46. Those who were blessed were those who cared and stood up for righteousness; those who ignored the needs of others, or maybe even added to them, were cursed.

Summary: Wisdom and Courage

Not all local beliefs are harmful, but many beliefs cause families to be marginalized, resulting in those with disability suffering negative effects on their lives and the lives of their families. It takes courage and wisdom from God to continue tirelessly helping the community to get rid of harmful beliefs while maintaining the valuable heritage from past generations.

7

Points of View

Eileen's Story

Eileen is a primary school teacher in a small town in Tanzania. She has two lovely daughters and is a member of the local Anglican Church. This sounds like a success story, but Eileen has stood in the face of many difficulties to achieve the life she now lives.

Eileen was the last-born of her family and is the only one born with albinism. Not long after her birth, her mother's struggles began. Her father's extended family refused to accept such a child into their family group, saying that Eileen could not be her father's daughter and that they would therefore reject her. Eileen's mother knew she had been faithful in her marriage, so the only option was for Eileen's mother to return to her family with Eileen, in a district some distance away.

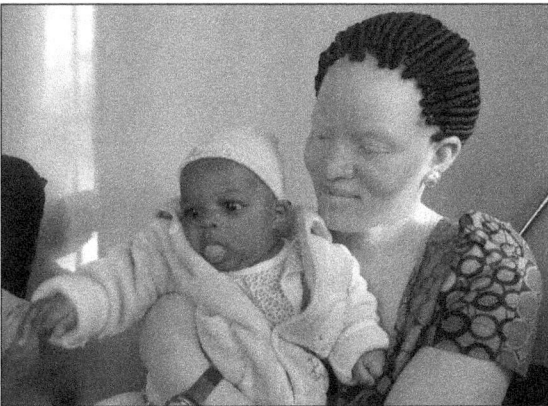

Figure 7.1. Eileen with her lovely daughter.
Photo ©Bridget Hathaway.

At school, Eileen was never chosen by the other pupils to be in their group, and if a pupil was asked to sit next to Eileen, he or she would take the first opportunity to run away. Thus Eileen often felt rejected and lonely. She would ask herself why she had all these problems, and she experienced a loss of self-confidence and self-respect as a result. To some extent she blamed herself for the challenges faced in the family. Thankfully, her mother gave Eileen wise counsel and stood by her throughout her formative years. After training to be a teacher, she got a job back in her home area.

Eileen acknowledges the changes in attitude that have taken place in the last few years in Tanzania. Now there is far less discrimination, and people accept her as they would accept anyone else. These changes are due, in part, to serious efforts by organizations of people with albinism that have raised awareness about albinism and advocated successfully for their right to live safely and to enjoy the same access to education, health care and social inclusion as everyone else. However, there are still many countries where people with albinism live in constant fear of their lives.

As Christians who follow the example of Christ, we should accept one another just as Christ accepted us, and work for justice for those whose lives have been affected by discrimination and rejection.

The Challenge of Acquired Disability

Pastor Mapinduzi is a determined and faithful pastor who has faced many challenges since he was ordained. He studied at theological college and completed his course along with the other students. Not long after his ordination, though, Pastor Mapinduzi began to have problems with his legs, feeling a tingling sensation leading to numbness and weakness. His ability to walk diminished until he could no longer stand without support. The local hospital failed to find the cause and X-rays seemed to show no abnormality. After another hospital visit resulted in no diagnosis, the extended family began to suspect that witchcraft was involved. It didn't seem to be a normal illness, so they believed he had an evil spirit. Eventually he was diagnosed with a prolapsed disc in his spine; this is a severe condition that can lead to total paralysis below the level of the affected disc. However, even after this diagnosis the family still believed that witchcraft was the cause, and it is possible they went to a traditional healer for advice. After further X-rays were taken that clearly showed the problem, and after spinal surgery, the family began to believe the true diagnosis. During this time, however, his first child was born with club feet. "Surely," people thought, "this proves he laughed at someone with disability, and that is why he and his child are disabled?" These were huge challenges for a young pastor, but he kept his faith throughout this time. Pastor Mapinduzi walks without a stick but he has balance problems, making it impossible for him to stand without support. Climbing steps is very difficult, and walking long distances is tiring and painful.

The diocese accepted his condition and he became a parish pastor. The evangelists agreed happily to his appointment, and, although initially congregations viewed him with some suspicion, this soon disappeared as they found he worked harder than most pastors without disability. However, there are many challenges for a pastor with a disability, and some of these arise even within the church service itself. Pastor Mapinduzi describes it this way:

> During a church service it is necessary to stand and sit at regular intervals, according to the instructions in the liturgy. If I sit instead of stand, the congregation find it difficult to understand, and feel the service isn't a "proper" service, particularly during the prayer of consecration. Physically, there are often many steps to be negotiated even before entering the church, then more steps to reach the altar and the place where the minister should be sitting. This is a challenge even before beginning the service.

Figure 7.2. Pastor Mapinduzi is an energetic and faithful pastor. Photo ©Bridget Hathaway.

An important part of any pastor's work is to make home visits to those who are in particular need or are bereaved. This work cannot be done by phone; culturally, it is essential for the pastor to visit personally. In a rural setting, this can be very challenging for someone with a disability, and sometimes it is impossible. This leads to some parishioners feeling he is not doing his job properly, despite their knowledge of his disability. He admitted that this attitude causes hurt. Regarding the administering of the Eucharist, Pastor Mapinduzi has resolved the problem. He remains by the altar and the congregation walk up to him in single file, so he need not descend the steps.

On a wider level, Pastor Mapinduzi shared some experiences he had in the community: "One day I was waiting by the roadside for a public transport taxi. I was using my crutches. A taxi came but drove straight past me, although there was space. Just ahead the taxi stopped for more passengers." When he arrived at his destination, Pastor Mapinduzi challenged the taxi driver that passed him. The assumption had been that as he was disabled, he wouldn't pay his fare because he must be poor. Thankfully, he met with a different attitude in the large city, where on four occasions when he offered the fare the driver wouldn't let him pay. "Perhaps they thought they would get a blessing by taking this attitude," Pastor Mapinduzi commented.

Section II

Disability and Theology: Completing the Body of Christ, the Church

Introduction to Section II

The emphasis in section I was predominantly medical, looking at different conditions that can affect people at some point in their lives. Although we touched on the question of how attitudes and beliefs can affect a person's everyday life, we did not focus on this in any depth. In section III we will look at the social and political aspects of disability, as it is important to understand these if we are to be an inclusive body of Christ. However, important though the medical and social/political aspects are, one foundational understanding of disability is missing: that of the person. Roy McCloughry writes on this point: "The medical model focuses on the physical body. The rights model focuses on the political body. What is needed is the missing *person.* It is this vacuum that the biblical picture seeks to fill."[1]

This section therefore looks at personhood, particularly from a theological perspective, using quotes from the Bible as well as from a variety of other writers, many of whom have personal experience of disability. As there is much to say about disability from a biblical perspective, and it can sometimes be controversial, all that follows is a mere taster of this broad subject.

---

1. Roy McCloughry, *The Enabled Life: Christianity in a Disabling World* (London: SPCK, 2013), 59.

8

What Is the Origin of Suffering and Disability?

In this chapter, we will look at some questions we need to think about when we are confronted with disability and suffering.

Is Disability a Punishment?

Have you ever heard someone talk about a child with disability and say something like this: "Ah, you know your sins will always come back to affect you. This child was born like that because of what Mama did earlier in her life. It's a punishment"? Do you think that might be true? What do you answer when someone with a disability says that to you? Or what do you say when a member of your congregation gives birth to a child who is blind, or deaf, or has twisted legs? What is your attitude when you lie awake at night thinking about what you can do to help someone with a disability? Or when you talk to other pastors and professionals working in the field of disability?

It is important that you consider your response to the question whether disability is a punishment before you have to confront it in real life, for it will affect how you respond to people with disabilities.

When we consider the idea of any kind of suffering being a punishment, we need to acknowledge that there are examples in the Bible that may support that viewpoint as well as examples that reject it. We cannot generalize these examples and say they apply to all situations. As pastors, we must consider both viewpoints in order to be true to the text.

The Viewpoint That Says "Disability Is Not a Punishment"

The Bible makes it clear that we are sinners and that our parents were sinners. If this is so, why were we not all born with disabilities? If we say that God punishes only some parents by sending them a child with a disability, we are saying that God treats some sins differently from others. Is this true? Surely all sin separates us from the God of love? God hates all sin, in all its forms, because his desire is to love and redeem all of his creation.

But, you may say, my sins are forgiven because I confessed them and trusted in Jesus. But did not the parents of the disabled child in your congregation do the same? Why are your sins forgiven and theirs are not?

Theologically, it makes no sense to say that God sends a disability as a punishment in an arbitrary fashion.

An Example from the New Testament

Let's look at this question by relying on the words and actions of Jesus himself when he healed a man who was born blind.

John 9 opens with the disciples asking a question that shows that they agree with the imaginary person we quoted at the start of this chapter: "Rabbi, who sinned, this man or his parents, that he was born blind?" (John 9:2). This was a common view at the time, just as it is a common view in Africa today. The disciples thought that the link between sin and suffering was so strong that a person might even be punished for some sin committed before he or she was born! The Pharisees certainly held this view too, for they told the man, "You were steeped in sin at birth" (9:34).

The argument in support of this view goes something like this: God is a God of justice; therefore, he does not allow something to happen that appears to us to be unjust, like an accident that leaves someone with a disability. If something like that happens, it probably means that some private sin is being punished. If we accept this argument, we feel that our just God is at work, and we feel more comfortable about the situation. In other words, we believe that God is justified in "punishing" the person because of an unconfessed sin.

But Jesus himself does not agree with this view! He responds to the disciples by saying, "Neither this man nor his parents sinned . . . but this happened so that the works of God might be displayed in him" (9:3).

The truth is that the world is complicated, and God's teaching is not always easy to understand; it can even be uncomfortable. As Tom Wright says, "We have to stop thinking of the world as a kind of moral slot-machine, where people put in a coin (a good act, say, or an evil one) and get out a particular result (a reward or a punishment)."[1]

Life in Christ is not one of reaping rewards for good deeds and receiving immediate punishment for bad deeds. However, as Wright explains, good and bad deeds can have decisive results: a kind and understanding attitude can bring peace in a situation, while stealing from someone can cause exclusion from the community.

There are clear examples of this in both the Old and New Testaments. In 2 Kings 5:15–27 we read of Elisha meeting with Naaman, who had leprosy. After Naaman was healed, Elisha refused any payment, but his servant Gehazi used deceit and lies to obtain gifts from Naaman. As a consequence, Gehazi was punished: "But Elisha said to him, 'Was not my spirit with you when the man got down from his chariot to meet you? Is this the time to take money or to accept clothes – or olive groves and vineyards, or flocks and herds, or male and female slaves? Naaman's leprosy will cling to you and to your descendants for ever.' Then Gehazi went from Elisha's presence and his skin was leprous – it had become as white as snow" (2 Kgs 5:26–17). Clearly the premeditated crime of Gehazi did not go unpunished: he was infected by Naaman's leprosy. The outcome would have affected his family too, because they would have lost the presence of Gehazi from their family unit when he was isolated for being a leper. Gehazi broke the tenth commandment by coveting riches rather than being honest.

In the New Testament we read in Acts 5:1–11 the story of Ananias and Sapphira, who deliberately cheated God by lying about the money they received from selling a plot of land. Peter tells Ananias, "'What made you think of doing such a thing? You have not lied just to human beings but to God.' When Ananias heard this, he fell down and died" (5:4b–5a).

In both these examples the offenders deepened their sin by continuing in their deceit and not repenting. The offence was judged and punished. However, this is quite different from saying that all disability is a result of sin. In both these cases there was deliberate sinning without repentance, and God, being a God of justice, must act justly.

Our position as children of God is purely due to the grace of God and the work Jesus did on the cross. The blind man in John's story is an example of God's desire to have each of us become a new creation. The man's blindness was not a punishment; quite the opposite: it was an opportunity for new creation.

---

1. Tom Wright, *John for Everyone: Part 1, Chapters 1–10* (London: SPCK; Louisville, KY: Westminster John Knox Press, 2002), 133–134.

Jesus used this man's blindness to teach his disciples a number of truths:

- The blindness was not a result of sin, but an opportunity for God's grace and compassion to be revealed in the healing of the man (John 9:3).
- While there is "light" (an opportunity), the work of God must be done because there may be a time when opportunities cease to be available (9:4).
- Jesus is the light of the world, and this act of healing supported his use of that metaphor and strengthened his claim to be the Son of God (9:5).
- Those who thought they could "see" (the Pharisees) were doubly guilty because while claiming to "see" they denied the truth. "Jesus said, 'If you were blind, you would not be guilty of sin; but now that you claim you can see, your guilt remains'" (9:41).

In this passage Jesus clearly dismisses the belief that disability happens because of sin.

There is one other point we need to notice from the passage. The blind man himself participated in the healing. He had to take some responsibility himself by making a choice to trust Jesus. But we are not told that he had to repent before he could be healed. In fact, there is no mention of the man himself talking about having sinned. What the man did was obey Jesus's instructions. Jesus did not just do something to him; he required a response of faith and action from the man. Sight and freedom came into the man's life as he believed in the Son of Man (9:35–38).

Can't God Prevent Suffering and Disability?

It sometimes seems that we are at the mercy of random natural events such as floods, earthquakes and lightning, or of disasters during pregnancy and childbirth that result in children having to live with severe disabilities. Why does God not intervene to prevent such things? Is it because he does not have the power to do so? If God is all-powerful (omnipotent), why is there pain, suffering and imperfection in the world?

These questions are difficult to answer. After all, we preach that God has conquered evil, yet there is still so much evil in the world. We may be tempted to doubt his power; maybe he is not omnipotent? But as Don Carson says, "To abandon belief in the omnipotence of God may 'solve' the problem of evil, but the cost is enormous: the resulting god is incapable of helping us."[2]

If God is not omnipotent, he cannot bring us comfort; he cannot answer prayers because he does not have the power to do so. The truth is that we do not know why God does not intervene every time we want him to. We are like David, who cried out, "How long, LORD? Will you forget me for ever?" (Ps 13:1). We need to face the fact that we may not have answers to all the questions we are asked, or that we ourselves ask. Yet this is not really surprising. How could God be God if we knew every answer to every question? We would no longer need him, for we would be small gods ourselves. The truth is well explained by Francis Bridger when he writes, "We are, until the Last Day, in-betweeners – people who inhabit an in-between land. We have neither completely escaped the pull of Good Friday not reached the glory of Easter Day."[3]

The God we serve is a mysterious God; we can never know everything about him. What is necessary is to continue to trust in his ultimate goodness and justice. "Now faith is confidence in what we hope for and assurance about what we do not see" (Heb 11:1).

Surely Christians Should Be Blessed?

There are those who claim that Christians who live in obedience to God will not suffer but will always enjoy the blessings of health, wealth and happiness. But when we study the Bible, we come across many faithful believers who suffered greatly, despite being committed to serving God. Think of men like Hosea, Jeremiah, Paul, Timothy and Job. Each of them suffered in different ways. Were any of them discarded from God's service because of their infirmity or disability? No, they all continued in their service in God's name. In fact, Paul puts it clearly in Philippians 3 when he says, "But whatever were gains to me I now consider loss for the sake of Christ. What is more, I consider everything a loss because of the surpassing worth of knowing Christ Jesus my Lord, for whose sake I have lost all things" (Phil 3:7–8a). He then continues, "I want to know Christ – yes, to know the power of his resurrection and participation in his sufferings . . . " (3:10a).

If God's servants like Paul and Job endured great suffering, do you still think that someone with a disability or that person's family must have done

---

2. D. A. Carson, *How Long, O Lord? Reflections on Suffering and Evil* (Nottingham: Inter-Varsity Press, 2006), 30.

3. Francis Bridger, *23 Days: A Story of Love, Death and God* (London: Darton, Longman & Todd, 2004), 95.

something wrong? What verse in the Bible suggests that as Christians we have a right to freedom from suffering and disability?

Surely Christians Should Be Perfect?

Perfection and Holiness

In Matthew 5:48 Jesus says, "Be perfect, therefore, as your heavenly Father is perfect." We know that he is talking about holiness, but maybe there is a part of us that assumes that the perfection he is talking about includes bodily perfection. So we sometimes equate holiness with perfection, and see a lack of perfection as a lack of holiness. There is no doubt that God has called us to be holy. But in the original Hebrew and Greek in which the Bible was written, being "holy" does not imply being perfect or whole in any physical sense; it means that we are set apart for God's service, set apart from worldly values and attitudes (1 Pet 1:13–16). We can be set apart or "holy" even when our bodies do not work like the majority of people's bodies. We can be "holy" even if our minds are not as active as other people's minds. God is not bound by the limitations we humans place on one another; he uses people as he chooses, in ways we may not understand.

Perfection and Creation

We may also want to stop and think about how we see perfection in relation to the world God created. How do we know that disability is not a part of the natural diversity God allows in this world? That is a startling thought! John Hull writes, "The idea of perfection, however, must be associated with the idea of diversity, for God's creation is perfect exactly in the extraordinary diversity of life."[4]

Good, Not Perfect

Let us look at the account of creation in Genesis 1. There we are told six times that God saw that what he had created "was good" (Gen 1:4, 10, 12, 18, 21, 25), and in Genesis 1:31 we read, "God saw all that he had made, and it was very good." This does not say that God saw that what he had made was perfect; it was very good. He was satisfied with what he had created. Maybe he even delighted in it!

---

4. John M. Hull, *Disability: The Inclusive Church Resource* (London: Darton, Longman & Todd, 2014), 84.

In His Image

The culmination of God's creative activity was the creation of a man and a woman, who were created in the image of God (Gen 1:27). But what exactly does this mean? There are many different ideas on this topic, ideas which are often influenced by the culture in which we are born and live.

One important clue to its meaning is found in Genesis 2:7, which reports a unique feature of the creation of human beings: "Then the LORD God formed a man from the dust of the ground and breathed into his nostrils the breath of life, and the man became a living being." We do not read of anything like that in God's creation of animals. Humans are unique in that God breathed "the breath of life" into them. The word translated "breath" can also be translated as "spirit," and it is the fact that we have God's spirit within us that enables us to have a relationship with God.

So how does this affect our attitude to people living with disability and the question as to whether God caused the disability to happen? Perhaps it helps us to realize that being created in the image of God has nothing to do with our appearance or our intellect. It has everything to do with God's spirit being breathed into us. Every human being has received this gift, and every human being can be in relationship with God. It is true that this relationship was disrupted when Adam and Eve sinned, but God is in the process of restoring this relationship in those who turn to him. Every single one of us is in the process of having our likeness to Christ restored. This is true whether we are able-bodied or not, for God's image is not physical but spiritual: "And we all, who with unveiled faces contemplate the Lord's glory, are being transformed into his image with ever-increasing glory, which comes from the Lord, who is the Spirit" (2 Cor 3:18). All of us are works in progress. Every one of us has imperfections that are being restored by the grace of God through the work of the Holy Spirit. Full restoration will only happen when we are with him for ever.

When we look at each other in this light, we do not see those with disabilities as "mistakes." No, we see them as people who are also made in God's image, and who are as valuable and cherished in God's sight as we are. John Hull, a theologian who lost his sight, wrote, "Disability is not something to be 'allowed for' or excused but something to be truly embraced. I say this not as part of some sort of secular equality agenda but because each person who crosses the threshold of the church, disabled or not, is made in the image of God and is to be regarded as precious for that reason."[5]

---

5. Hull, *Disability*, 37–38.

Perhaps we should approach the question as to why God allows disabilities from a different angle and ask: Why are we reluctant to face the truth that the world is not perfect?

Summary

Let us sum up the answers to the questions we have explored in this chapter:

- Is disability necessarily a punishment for sin? No, because Jesus explicitly denies this, and because we have all sinned yet we do not all have disability.
- Can God intervene in suffering, or are we at the mercy of the randomness of the world? If we think that the randomness of the world causes our suffering, we deny that God is omnipotent. If we deny God's omnipotence, we reduce his power so that he also becomes subject to the world's unpredictability.
- Do we have a right to live free from suffering and disability? If we say yes, on what biblical text do we base this claim?
- Is suffering a sign that we are cursed? Many Bible characters who suffered in various ways had not committed significant sins. They were not discarded from God's service or cursed; rather, they played an important part in God's plan of salvation.
- Shouldn't Christians be perfect? In the creation story God never mentions perfection. He created humankind in his own image. Does that mean that someone with a disability is a mistake? No, that is a purely external judgment; being made in God's image is more than external.
- So what does it mean to be made in God's image? Being made in God's image means having the breathed-in spirit of God that opens the way to a unique relationship with God. The image of God in us is not physical but spiritual. We are all equal in the sight of God.

You are worthy, our Lord and God,
>   to receive glory and honour and power,
> for you created all things,
>>   and by your will they were created
>>   and have their being.
>   (Rev 4:11)

9

Disability and Healing

A Story

Pastor Emmanuel's church was in a suburban area not far from a large town. He enjoyed pastoring his lively congregation and was delighted to have a Sunday school of nearly seventy children. His youth choir had gone from strength to strength, although he sometimes had to keep an eye on the young men!

Once a month the church held a healing service, when anyone who felt the need of God's healing hand could come and be prayed for by a small team of people. On one occasion, a faithful member of the congregation brought her daughter Francesca to the service. Few people had ever met Francesca as she never came to church; she was severely disabled with cerebral palsy and was kept at home most of the time. When Francesca was wheeled to the front in her wheelchair, a member of the healing team asked Mama Francesca what she would like prayer for. "I want Francesca to walk and be like other girls of her age," she said. A member of the prayer team began praying, beginning quietly, asking for God's healing for Francesca. Gradually his voice grew louder until he was shouting and waving his arms, pleading with God to forgive the sins of mother and daughter and to make Francesca whole. Francesca continued to sit in her wheelchair, clearly afraid. Eventually the prayer ended. There was a short pause, then the team member said, "There is a sin one of you has not confessed. God cannot heal when you are not repentant. Go away and ask God to reveal the sin to you, so that you can repent."

Feeling full of shame, Mama Francesca went home, wheeling her daughter slowly along the dusty street. "I know I sin," she said to herself, "but I always ask for God's forgiveness. I do my best with Francesca, I love her and care for her, and she cannot have done wrong. How can I return to church when people think I am sinful?"

When Mama Francesca did not attend church for several Sundays, Pastor Emmanuel went to visit her. Reluctantly, Mama Francesca explained why she had stayed away. Gently, the pastor took her hand, and said, "Let's pray for God's peace, blessing and love to fill your heart and the heart of Francesca." He then prayed; beautifully and sincerely he asked for God's healing presence in the heart of every member of the household. Mama Francesca felt a strange warmth enter her heart; her entire body felt as if it was ready to burst with thankfulness. "What is happening?" she whispered. Pastor Emmanuel replied, "You are both being healed."

This story covers a variety of points that we need to consider when thinking about healing ministry. We will examine these points below.

In this chapter we will confine our study to healing in connection with disability. We will not look at every aspect of healing, as that would take a whole book in itself!

Cure or Healing?

The first point we need to consider is in connection with the two words "cure" and "healing." These words are frequently used in connection with illness or disability, but is there a difference in meaning between them?

The *Oxford English Dictionary* defines the meaning of the verb "to cure" as "to eliminate a disease, condition or injury with medical treatment."[1] However, "to heal" is defined as "to cause a wound, injury or person to become sound or healthy again. Restore to sound health."[2] In the first instance, that of "cure," there is a total removal or reversal of the person's present health problem through the use of medical treatment. With regard to healing, the whole person is mentioned, described as being "restore[d] to sound health." Medical intervention is not mentioned. Being restored to sound health is more than a physical restoration and includes mental, emotional and spiritual well-being. Indeed, physical restoration might not actually be included since medical treatment is not necessarily a part of healing. The word "restoration" is important here, as it implies a renewing of an aspect of a person's life. One aspect of the renewing might be that the person is returned to full participation in the community in which he or she had been marginalized. In Luke 8 we see an example of this. Jesus healed a man who was demon-possessed by casting

---

1. Judy Pearsall and Patrick Hanks, eds., *The New Oxford Dictionary of English* (Oxford: OUP, 1998), 450.

2. Pearsall and Hanks, *New Oxford Dictionary*, 846.

the demons into a herd of pigs. Jesus then told the man to return home and tell how much God had done for him. "So the man went away and told all over the town how much Jesus had done for him" (Luke 8:39b). Similarly, writing of Jesus's healing miracles in Luke 5:12–26 in the *Africa Bible Commentary*, Paul John Isaak says, "For such individuals, being healed means being restored to one's extended family, friends and community. Health, therefore, implies safe integration into the life of society."[3]

Any conversation about healing must therefore include the family and community from which the person comes. A person who is not restored to his or her family and community is unlikely to be fully healed. Western society has focused more on curing a person, forgetting that the support of and integration in the family and community is an important part of health and well-being.

It is possible for a person to be cured but not healed. For example, imagine a young woman who has a severe limp as a result of a faulty injection she was given when she was a child. After an operation she is able to walk normally again. However, she remains angry and bitter, and has no peace in her life. Her attitude causes her to be marginalized in the community. She has been cured but, according to the above definition, she has not been healed.

Likewise, a person could be healed but not cured. Imagine that a young man loses a leg in an accident. While in hospital a nurse tells him about Jesus, and the young man reads his Bible and gives his life to Jesus. His disability remains, but he receives peace and a purpose for his life despite the disability. His positive and caring attitude means that he is accepted in the community. He has not been cured, but he has been healed.

Healing and Cure in the Bible

Is the difference in meaning between healing and cure found in the Bible? If we look at accounts of Jesus's healing ministry in the New Testament, we find that different words are used in the original Greek for "healing," "cleansed" and "cure." For example, in Luke 17:11–19 we read of ten lepers who were cleansed from their leprosy, but only one of whom returned to thank Jesus. In verse 14, the Greek word used has the meaning of being "cleansed." In verse 15, the one leper who returned saw that he had been "cured" (a different Greek word), and in verse 19, Jesus tells him he has been "healed" (another word again in the Greek). Three different words are used with specific meanings to clarify

---

3. In Tokunboh Adeyemo, ed., *Africa Bible Commentary* (Nairobi: Word Alive; Grand Rapids, MI: Zondervan, 2006), 1214, para. 3.

the point being made by Jesus.[4] Rev Dr Anthony Bird describes it this way: "In Christian (but not only Christian) thought wholeness or healing is union with God and we see that being cured is not the same as being healed: ten lepers were cured, but only one of them healed."[5]

In Luke 13:10–16 we read of a crippled woman being healed. In verse 14 the synagogue leader is "indignant because Jesus had healed on the Sabbath," and the Greek word used here is the meaning "healed," not "cured." The woman received more than a cure. Jesus said, "Then should not this woman, a daughter of Abraham, whom Satan has kept bound for eighteen long years, be set free on the Sabbath day from what bound her?" (13:16). The woman had been set free from her physical limitations to live a full life in the community. However, is it not also possible that she had been set free spiritually, too, from "what bound her"?

Healing Then and Now

People sometimes ask, "Why is it that so many healings took place in New Testament times and so few happen in our day?" That is a good question to discuss! Here are a few thoughts that may help the discussion.

Although the focus of some healing miracles in the New Testament was exclusively on the person in need, many miracles took place with an audience. These miracles might be said to have had a two-fold purpose. Jesus certainly had compassion on the person in need, but it is possible he was also using the occasion to make a point to the audience around him. Perhaps through the healing he was revealing to them the truth of who he was: the Son of God.

In Mark 2:1–12, for example, we read of the healing of the paralysed man. Jesus says to him, "Son, your sins are forgiven" (2:5b). We already know from the text that the room was full of visitors, including teachers of the law. Jesus knew they did not believe who he was, so he used the occasion to provoke a reaction from them. He did not accuse the paralysed man of specific sin, but his general comment regarding forgiveness of sin was enough to challenge the unbelief of the Jewish leaders. The response of the leaders provided an opportunity for Jesus to declare who he was: "the Son of Man" (v. 10). The man was healed, but in addition the crowd and teachers of the law witnessed Jesus declaring his true identity.

---

4. Alfred Marshall, *The NIV Interlinear Greek–English New Testament* (Grand Rapids, MI: Zondervan, 1976), 314.

5. Anthony Bird, *The Search for Health: A Response from the Inner City* (UK: University of Birmingham, Institute for the Study of Worship and Religious Architecture, 1982), 104.

Where Do Our Beliefs about Healing Come From?

Our beliefs about healing may come from one or more of the following sources:

- As Christians, some of our beliefs about healing will come from the Bible, from both Old and New Testament accounts of healing.
- Some of our attitudes about healing will come from the culture in which we live.
- Different faith groups have different beliefs about healing.
- Our beliefs about healing may have been affected by personal experience of a healing ministry.

You might be able to add other ideas to this list. We looked at beliefs and attitudes in chapter 6.

So What Are You Hoping for When You Pray for Healing?

This is an important question, and it might be helpful for you to write down your answer or discuss it with others.

- Perhaps you are hoping for healing in a specific way. In the story at the start of the chapter, Mama Francesca wanted prayer on behalf of her daughter so that she might be able to walk and be like other girls of her age. She was hoping for Francesca to be cured.
- Perhaps you know of someone who has seizures (epilepsy) and you ask for prayer that the seizures might cease so that your friend can live free of this problem.
- Maybe your prayer is for someone you have heard about from friends, not someone personally known to you, who is suffering in some way.

In all these cases there is one common factor: the desire is for physical cure, for visible change to take place.

Of course God can heal physically; but what happens when he does not do so?

Healed without Physical Change

In the earlier story, Mama Francesca was hoping for a physical change in her daughter's body. Even the healing team member who was praying for her probably expected to see Francesca stand up and walk away. But Francesca was not cured; she remained sitting in her wheelchair. Was this a failure?

Was there a reason why Francesca was not cured? The healing team member thought there was a reason for this lack of visible change, and said it was unconfessed sin. The following words were written by a parent of a child with disability: "When the expected cure fails to occur, the marked person is further blamed (not necessarily overtly) for the failure: too little faith, too little prayer, too much of a sinner. Not only does the disability persist, but he or she has disappointed the community by not being miraculously cured."[6]

As we read in the story, Mama Francesca walked home feeling full of shame for the lack of change in Francesca. The expectations of others and her own feeling of shame added to her problems. She returned home worse off than if she had never gone for prayer. Is that kind of outcome honouring to God? Is it not, in fact, a form of spiritual abuse of a vulnerable person? If the answer is "Yes, it is abuse," how should we, as church leaders, handle this type of situation? Abuse is a serious matter that brings condemnation on the church. We should never cause people to leave the church in a worse state than when they arrived; if we do, we have dishonoured God. Thankfully, Pastor Emmanuel understood that healing may take a form other than physical healing; he realized that God would look at Mama Francesca's inner needs and touch her where she most needed healing.

In 2 Corinthians 12:7b–10 we read of Paul suffering a "thorn in the flesh." While we do not know what that was – whether it was a physical ailment or something else – we do know that, after praying three times for it to be removed, Paul remained with this limiting factor in his life. It was not a failure on Paul's part; he does not seek out a sinful cause for it – quite the opposite. He says, "But he [the Lord] said to me, 'My grace is sufficient for you, for my power is made perfect in weakness.' Therefore I will boast all the more gladly about my weaknesses, so that Christ's power may rest on me" (12:9).

For Paul, weakness in his body gave God the opportunity to show his purpose and power in Paul's life. Many people living with disability would probably choose to be able-bodied, but God uses people with disability in his work just as he uses people without disability. The greatest limitation comes not from God, but from society; sadly, society often judges in a negative way, seeing what people cannot do, instead of looking at their abilities.

In the Old Testament, when Samuel was choosing the king to replace Saul, he asked Jesse's sons to walk before him. Samuel thought he knew which son was most suited to be king: Eliab looked healthy and physically strong. But

---

6. Myroslaw Tataryn and Maria Truchan-Tataryn, *Discovering Trinity in Disability* (New York: Orbis, 2013), 98.

Samuel was wrong: "The LORD said to Samuel, 'Do not consider his appearance or his height, for I have rejected him. The LORD does not look at the things people look at. People look at the outward appearance, but the LORD looks at the heart'" (1 Sam 16:7).

Are We Searching for "Normality"?

Sometimes in the church we imitate the "medical model" in our healing ministries. This means we look for *cure* in a situation, for restoration to "normality." This leads us to another question: What do we mean by "normality"? It may be that the idea of "normality" is something that we human beings have constructed. God creates each person as a unique child of his; he enjoys the diversity of his creation, seeing each person as special, whatever their ability or disability.

> You have searched me, LORD,
>   and you know me . . .
> For you created my inmost being;
>   you knit me together in my mother's womb.
> I praise you because I am fearfully and wonderfully made;
>   your works are wonderful,
>   I know that full well.
> (Ps 139:1, 13–14)

When we pray expecting cure, perhaps we are limiting God to working within our human ideas; but God is infinitely greater than this. Instead of focusing on a person's disability we can seek the image of God in that person. When we do this, we are more likely to pray for the best for that person, rather than for what we think he or she needs. After all, as we discussed in chapter 9, being created in God's image is about having God's breathed-in spirit within us, rather than being created in physical likeness.

Beware of Assumptions!

You may be the pastor of a church or an evangelist, or you may be training to be a church leader with responsibility for many different aspects of ministry, including healing. When you offer prayer for healing it is important that you beware of making assumptions.

For example, are you sure you know why a particular person has come forward for healing? Imagine the following situation.

A member of your congregation who walks with crutches comes forward when prayer for healing is offered. "O Lord," the lay leader cries, "have mercy on this servant of yours and heal her. Take away the spirit of lameness . . . " Later, the member who was prayed for shares her story with you, the pastor or evangelist, explaining, "I came forward on behalf of my neighbour who is seriously sick in hospital, to ask for prayer for her. I am not in need of healing at the moment; I am healthy! But the lay leader never gave me a chance to explain!" An assumption was made that because the church member had a disability, she would want "healing." If the person coming forward for prayer had been able-bodied, would we have made an assumption about her need?

Are You Unique?

You were born with a certain shape to your face: it may be slightly long, or rather round; your eyes might be quite close together or far apart. This is part of who you are, your uniqueness. Likewise, a person might be born with an arm, leg or one side of his or her body paralysed. That person is used to being like this and has never known anything different. Some disabled people feel that when you pray for them to become whole, you are actually taking away part of their identity. The person they are includes being paralysed on one side, being hearing-impaired or having a learning impairment. Praying for these people to be "cured" of their disability implies that they are not acceptable as they are, and takes away their identity.

However, it would be wrong to assume that all people with disabilities think in this way. Some long for a cure, to be free from their disabilities, free from discomfort and rejection. Some families, whose lives are given to caring for those with disabilities, pray constantly for relief from their caring responsibilities. These people would choose a cure for their family members. But we should not assume that a change in their bodies is what people with disability desire.

Summary

We have discussed many things in this chapter. We have looked at the difference between healing and cure, and how this is approached in the Bible. We have considered Bible texts in relation to apparent lack of physical change after prayer, and we have wondered about normality and uniqueness in human creation.

At the end of all our study we return to Jesus and his example as the Son of God. In Luke 5 we read of Jesus meeting with a man suffering from leprosy.

The leper begged Jesus to heal him: "When he saw Jesus, he fell with his face to the ground and begged him, 'Lord, if you are willing, you can make me clean.' Jesus reached out his hand and touched the man. 'I am willing,' he said. 'Be clean!' And immediately the leprosy left him" (Luke 5:12b–13).

The amazing point here is not so much the healing as the action of Jesus: "Jesus reached out and touched the leper. That was a radical step demonstrated by Jesus. Jesus need not have touched him – but he did – to break ritual taboos that kept people apart. Social barriers need to be broken down if true healing is to take place."[7]

The challenge is this: Are we ready to break down social barriers and taboos as Jesus did?

7. Wati Longchar, in *Sprouts of Disability Theology*, ed. Christopher Rajkumar (Nagpur, India: National Council of Churches in India, 2012), 40.

10

God-Enabled:
Meeting Some Bible Characters

Jars of Clay

> For God, who said, "Let light shine out of darkness," made his light shine in our hearts to give us the light of the knowledge of God's glory displayed in the face of Christ. But we have this treasure in jars of clay to show that this all-surpassing power is from God and not from us. (2 Cor 4:6–7)

We have already looked at the fact that we are made in the image of God, and that this has more to do with relationship than it does with any physical likeness. Here we look at some characters in the Bible whose relationships and identity were strengthened by God despite their feelings of inadequacy.

In Exodus 3 we read of God appearing to Moses. This was a key moment for Moses, a moment when God revealed himself by name. Perhaps when we read of God's self-declaration, it is also a key moment for us. Moses was chosen by God for a mighty purpose: to lead the Israelites out of slavery to the land promised to them by God. Was Moses excited about this task? No, he was distinctly reluctant! Knowing that Moses needed personal reassurance, God introduced himself by name: "God said to Moses, 'I AM WHO I AM. This is what you are to say to the Israelites: "I AM [Yahweh] has sent me to you" (Exod 3:14).

Names are extremely important. As John Goldingay writes, "As a human being I can be described by means of a list of characteristics – such as enthusiastic, imaginative, colourful, physical and unassuming . . . Yet such lists do not satisfactorily sum up the person."[1] Are we ever guilty of describing someone as "that man with one arm" or "that girl who doesn't understand/ talk"? When, however, you use the person's name, such as Peter or Susanna, that person becomes an individual; you are affirming who he or she is. And God knows you and me by name.

You, with your personality, your physical attributes and your name, make up a unique combination that is not repeated in anyone else. God knew that Moses needed this personal encounter with him, using God's own name, Yahweh. Why was Moses lacking in confidence? Because he had a speech impediment and doubted his own ability: "Moses said to the LORD, 'Pardon your servant, LORD. I have never been eloquent, neither in the past nor since you have spoken to your servant. I am slow of speech and tongue" (Exod 4:10). The Lord's anger was aroused when Moses persisted in avoiding God's call on his life; however, the anger was mainly due to the fact that Moses could see only his disability and doubted that God could use him, while God saw beyond the disability to Moses's ability, wisdom and perseverance. Having a name' gives us a distinct identity and opens up possibilities. Do you remember how God called Adam in Genesis 3:9? It was as if God was calling him by name, saying, "Adam, Adam, where are you?" And in Isaiah 43:1b God says, "Fear not, for I have redeemed you; I have called you by name, you are mine" (ESV).

Jacob had a mixed history. Having cheated his brother Esau of his father's blessing kept for the firstborn son, Jacob spent an unsettled time in fear of Esau's reaction when they met again. But God had a plan for Jacob that would change history. In Genesis 32 we read of a personal meeting between "a man" and Jacob. Although there is no certainty as to the identity of the "man," many commentators agree that he was likely to have been God appearing in human form.[2] The "man" asked for Jacob's name, thus identifying him as an individual; he then gave Jacob a new name, and a new purpose which was related to his new name. Jacob became Israel: "Then the man said, 'Your name will no longer be Jacob, but Israel, because you have struggled with God and with humans and have overcome'" (Gen 32:28).

Jacob was left with a reminder of his struggle; his hip was damaged and he remained with a limp. This was a reminder of victory, of a profound change for Jacob – not only his change of name but also his legacy: that he would be

1. John Goldingay, in *Encounter with Mystery: Reflections on L'Arche and Living with Disability*, ed. Frances Young (London: Darton, Longman & Todd, 1997), 138.

2. See e.g. Gordon Wenham, *Genesis 16–50*, Word Biblical Commentary (Dallas: Word, 1994), 296; James McKeown, *Genesis*, Two Horizons OT Commentary (Grand Rapids, MI: Eerdmans, 2008), 154.

the ancestor of a nation and a community of nations (Gen 35:11). Far from the disability being a negative attribute for Jacob, it became his identity as the one who overcame.

Was Christ Disabled?

> Surely he took up our pain
>   and bore our suffering,
> yet we considered him punished by God,
>   stricken by him, and afflicted.
> But he was pierced for our transgressions,
>   he was crushed for our iniquities;
> the punishment that brought us peace was on him,
>   and by his wounds we are healed.
> (Isa 53:4–5)

Isaiah paints a vivid picture of the suffering servant. He is pierced, crushed both physically and mentally; he is wounded. This picture is of a Christ that we sometimes choose to forget. Christ was permanently scarred, for all to behold, and yet we all too often read the New Testament from an able-bodied viewpoint. We may even view people with disability as being less than the perfection we think God desires; yet can this be true? From the cradle to the grave Jesus was subject to rejection, was despised and was stigmatized. The word "stigmata" means cuts or brandings of the skin, often in order to mark a person out as unacceptable; it resulted in permanent scarring. Jesus was permanently scarred after the crucifixion, as the Gospel writers noted: "Jesus came and stood among them and said, 'Peace be with you!' After he said this, he showed them his hands and side. The disciples were overjoyed when they saw the Lord . . . But he [Thomas] said to them, 'Unless I see the nail marks in his hands and put my finger where the nails were, and put my hand into his side, I will not believe'" (John 20:19b, 20, 25).

These post-crucifixion scars were not hidden; Jesus asked his disciples to touch them. This not only allowed the disciples to believe that Christ had indeed risen from the dead, but it also restored to Jesus his humanity, the human touch that is so important in a caring relationship. Are there times when we are afraid to touch someone with a disability, particularly those who are non-verbal and we find it hard to relate to? In Isaiah 49:15–16a God says he has written our names on the palms of his hands. Does this mean he has written our names across the scars by which he saved us? If so, we are integrally part of that suffering and the suffering of others for whom Jesus died. As John Hull writes, "According to Christian faith the saving reality of God in Christ was not his immediate and brilliant perfection but his emptying."[3]

The following verses bring us face to face with one aspect of Jesus's character and ministry: "Have this mind among yourselves, which is yours in Christ Jesus, who, though he was in the form of God, did not count equality with God a thing to be grasped, but emptied himself, taking the form of a servant, being born in the likeness of men. And being found in human form he humbled himself and became obedient unto death, even death on a cross" (Phil 2:5–8 RSV). Jesus was "in the form of God" yet emptied himself of godly attributes by taking human form, accepting the humble role of a servant. It is a paradox that in the final hours before the crucifixion it was the vulnerability of Jesus that won him the victory. It was a time when human strength was at an end, and the mighty work of God was to be made manifest.

In what way does this relate to our thoughts about the church and people with disability? Perhaps it brings us back to the verse quoted at the beginning of this chapter. The treasure of God's presence in us, his light of salvation, is kept in our vulnerable bodies, described in 2 Corinthians 4 as "jars of clay." It is not human strength that counts, it is not high intellect (although both of these might be useful); rather it is Christ working through our vulnerability and weakness that enables his light to shine in strength. When we think negatively about people because of their disabilities, are we not forgetting that we are all "jars of clay" yet able to be used by God? God still redeems us in love despite our vulnerability.

Job and His "Comforters"

One of the characters in the Bible that we most connect with difficulties is Job. When we are introduced to him he has great wealth, is blessed with many children and appears to have a life that some people would think was perfect. God then permits the devil to test Job to the utmost, to see if he will deny God. Job's friends visit him and listen to him as he laments the very day of his birth and longs for God to take his life (Job 3 and 6). Unfortunately, instead of allowing Job to pour out his feelings, his friends make the judgment that he must have sinned, and that his suffering is God's discipline (see e.g. Job 4). We know this is not true because of what we read in Job chapters 1 and 2. In Job

---

3. John M. Hull, *Disability: The Inclusive Church Resource* (London: Darton, Longman & Todd, 2014), 87.

2:3 we read, "Then the LORD said to Satan, 'Have you considered my servant Job? There is no one on earth like him; he is blameless and upright, a man who fears God and shuns evil. And he still maintains his integrity, though you incited me against him to ruin him without any reason.'" Job's friends expect an attitude of penitence and pretence that is unhealthy and not justified since God has declared Job blameless.

Likewise, as a church leader, you will confront situations in which people are suffering greatly. To respond by simply saying, "Praise God in all things" does not recognize the humanity of these people. Lament is a strong element in the Psalms, where David voiced his agonies. Alison Lo writes, "Advocating upbeat and triumphalist worship amidst dismay is unhealthy. . . . Lament needs a voice and shouldn't be bottled up."[4] Even Christ cried out to his Father: "About three in the afternoon Jesus cried out in a loud voice, '*Eli, Eli, lema sabachthani*?' (which means 'My God, my God, why have you forsaken me?')" (Matt 27: 46).

Pouring out our heartache and pain to God can bring healing and peace to our spirits and quieten our souls to listen to God. However, some people may need guidance to come out of the lament into a place of peace with God. Do not hurry them, but instead gently guide people in this direction when they are ready for it. As a pastor, being able to listen to people in their laments is an important skill for successful God-centred ministry.

Valuing Our Brothers and Sisters

Parents who are responsible for severely disabled children face many hard questions regarding the future care and love of their children. In *Discovering Trinity in Disability*, the authors write of their concerns about their disabled daughter:

> So where do we Christians belong? Or more to the point, to what community do we want to belong? We are in the world but are we of the world? The world devalues Aleksandra [their daughter]: she will not work (generate income), vote (fulfil a civic duty), feed herself (experience autonomy). The world's standards say she is a burden on society. But what about the church? Will Aleksandra know acceptance for who she is? Will there be a community of

---

4. Alison Lo, in *Encounter with God* (Bible Notes), 13 July 2018 (Milton Keynes: Scripture Union), 19.

respect and support when we, her parents, die? Or will she become invisible because she is a failed miracle?[5]

Aleksandra's parents make the point that if Christians are a "holy" people, set apart for God's work, then the attitudes of the world are not always our attitudes, the values of the world are not our values and the behaviour of the world is not our behaviour. We are different. We are to welcome into relationship those whom society rejects, just as Jesus did, shocking the leaders by breaking long-held traditions. As Manchala writes, "As the gospels tell us, Jesus did not commission his disciples to call people to a belief system but a covenantal relationship through a vocation of striving for the realization of God's reign."[6]

As Christians we welcome and realize God's reign on earth, not by devaluing people, but by the way we live in relationship with all people. In Luke 4:18 Jesus, quoting from Isaiah 61:1–2, spoke these words: "The Spirit of the Lord is on me, because he has anointed me to proclaim good news to the poor. He has sent me to proclaim freedom for the prisoners, and recovery of sight for the blind, to set the oppressed free, to proclaim the year of the Lord's favour." Perhaps, instead of thinking literally of prisoners in gaol and people who are physically blind, we should also understand this as a call for those of us who are believers to be freed from attitudes that imprison marginalized people in their condition, which includes people with disability. Instead, we should build on this covenantal relationship with Jesus.

Summary

If we worship a triune God, we are already worshipping a God who is alive in relationship by the very nature of who he is. That being so, is it not true that we are built for relationship? And if we deny the opportunity of relationship to someone, then are we not also denying, to some degree, the very nature of God: Father, Son and Holy Spirit? This is a relationship of love.

---

5. Myroslaw Tataryn and Maria Truchan-Tataryn, *Discovering Trinity in Disability* (New York: Orbis, 2013), 89.

6. Deenabandhu Manchala, "Moving in the Spirit: Called to Transforming Discipleship," *International Review of Mission* 106, no. 2 (December 2017): 201.

11

What Does It Mean to Be Human?

Created to Be in Relationship with God

Have you ever thought about what it means to be human? On one level, we can look at the physical aspect of a human being and see clearly the differences between an animal and a human being. However, if we locate humanity purely in physicality, we create a model that is likely to be based on "normality," with anything else being viewed as "deviant."

In Genesis 1:27 we read that humankind is made in the image of God. We cannot limit our understanding of God to physical form; being made in the image of God is not physical, but relational, as we explored in chapter 9. The real difference between a human being and other forms of life is, therefore, far deeper and more complicated than purely the physical. An understanding of what it is to be human is likely to affect the way we treat other people, and, in the context of disability, it may affect our attitudes to our brothers and sisters who are living with disability, and consequently the way we treat them. The idea that relationship and being human are inseparable is a major theme in Dr Rowan Williams's book *Being Human*. Writing that our foundational relationship is with God, he says, "So . . . , before anything else happens I am in relation to a non-worldly, non-historical everlasting attention and love, which is God."[1]

If our first relationship is with God by the very fact of our creation, that means there is a sacred place in each human being where God dwells. People might not recognize God within them, but the fact remains that God created

---

1. Rowan Williams, *Being Human: Bodies, Minds, Persons* (London: SPCK, 2018), 36–37.

them to have relationship with him. Williams adds, "That means that there's a very serious limit on my freedom to make of my neighbour what I choose, because, to put it very bluntly, they don't belong to me, and their relation to me is not all that is true of them, or even the most important thing that is true of them."[2]

In other words, in the context of disability, when I meet a person whose understanding of the world is limited, I am not at liberty to judge that person as an inferior human being; God has already laid claim on that person as of value and loved. The nature of that person's relationship with me is only a part of who he or she is; the greater part is that person's relationship with God. In the context of people with profound intellectual impairment, Roy McCloughry quotes Dietrich Bonhoeffer as writing: "Life created and preserved by God possesses an inherent right; completely independent of its social utility . . . There is no worthless life before God, because God holds life itself to be valuable. Because God is the Creator, Preserver and Redeemer of life, even the poorest life before God becomes a valuable life."[3]

Human beings have certain basic needs that are universal. No matter how severely disabled people might be, to deny them their basic needs is to deny them their humanity. Among these basic needs is the need for love. To deny love and respect to someone is to ignore their worth as a human being. Jesus himself is our model; he showed love and compassion to those whom others rejected.

When we regard other people as less than human we place a barrier between them and ourselves, and this barrier may allow us to ignore them, or treat them badly, without feeling guilty. It allows us to argue that different standards can be applied to them. Is it possible that this occurs in our attitude to brothers and sisters living with disability – especially people with learning impairment – even within Christian circles? As human beings in relationship with God, we have a responsibility to treat one another with dignity; if we neglect to do so, we fail to honour God in other people. This is something we should remember when we feel inclined to treat other people dishonourably because they are different from us.

---

2. Williams, *Being Human*, 37.

3. Roy McCloughry, *The Enabled Life: Christianity in a Disabling World* (London: SPCK, 2013), 41.

Valued in Community

To be valued is an important part of being human. If we feel we have no worth, we feel that there is little point in life. We cannot be valued without being in relationship, so the concept of community, of belonging somewhere, brings the stability in which we can grow and flourish as human beings. Although it is true that God values and loves us unconditionally, it is hard for us to understand that without it being channelled through other people. When we, as Christians, value and care for one another, we are reflecting that relational aspect of God's nature. This is often reciprocal; we are a channel for the acceptance and valuing of someone, but we also receive the same from that person. It is not one-sided. However, when someone is not valued, but is denied relationship and a sense of belonging, they may fall into a dark depression – especially if they have no verbal language, as may be the case with those who have more profound disabilities. They still have feelings, are still aware of love, security and belonging, even if they cannot express that awareness. Belonging brings healing; as our relationship with another person grows, so the disabilities within us both diminish, bringing mutual healing and growth. Here we are not talking of physical healing, but emotional and spiritual healing. When we experience a sense of belonging, of relationship with another person, growth in confidence is more likely to take place. Growth and change are integral to what it is to be human. If we stifle the growth of a person through lack of belonging, lack of caring and lack of recognizing gifts, the humanity of that person is also stifled. Williams writes, "I'm a person because I am spoken to, I'm attended to, and I'm spoken and attended and loved into actual existence."[4]

Perhaps at this point we need to ask ourselves a difficult question: Why is it that so few people with disability are found in our churches? This is not just about physical disability, but every kind of disability, including the "invisible" disabilities such as epilepsy or mental illness. Initially, we may seek easy explanations: it is physically hard to get to church, there is no one to accompany them, or maybe we think that there are few people with disability living in our parishes. However, if we are honest, the real explanation is probably very different.

Cultures and societies are changing today far more rapidly than in the past, largely as a result of social media and global communication bringing new ideas into communities. Societal change is communal; but people with disability, if

---

4. Williams, *Being Human*, 45.

they are not integrated into communities, including the church community, are excluded from the changes taking place and become increasingly marginalized.

The Church as Community

If one element of being human is that of belonging, of being in human relationship with other people, the next step from this is that of inclusion into a group, whatever that group might be. If the group, or community, is the church, then including people with disability into the life of the church is a recognition of their humanity. This inclusion recognizes their gifts, what they can offer to the development of the church, as well as what we can give to them. Speaking particularly of people with intellectual impairment, Amos Yong writes: "How might the church begin to realise the power of the gospel in the lives of people with intellectual disabilities so that we consider not only ministry *to* such people but also ministry *with* them?"[5]

Every human being has a unique personality. As we read in Psalm 139,

> For you created my inmost being;
>   you knit me together in my mother's womb.
> I praise you because I am fearfully and wonderfully made;
>   your works are wonderful,
>   I know that full well.
> (Ps 139:13–14)

When we take away the freedom for someone to develop physically, spiritually, emotionally and socially, we take away that person's freedom to become fully human. We do not always realize when we are limiting someone's freedom; but when we, as a church, do not offer a hand of acceptance and love to a brother or sister living with disability, we are, in fact, limiting their freedom. The UN Convention on the Rights of Persons with Disabilities[6] makes it clear in many of its Articles that people with disability have the right to freedom in every area of their lives (see, for example, Articles 9, 14, 15, 16 and many others). This includes the right to participate in the activities of society. If we inhibit a person's freedom, are we not also inhibiting our own freedom? As Nelson Mandela famously said: "I am not truly free if I am taking away

---

5. Amos Yong, *The Bible, Disability, and the Church: A New Vision of the People of God* (Grand Rapids: Eerdmans, 2011), 111.

6. "Convention on the Rights of Persons with Disabilities (CRPD)," United Nations, accessed 4 January 2019, https://www.un.org/development/desa/disabilities/convention-on-the-rights-of-persons-with-disabilities.html.

someone else's freedom, just as surely as I am not free when my freedom is taken from me . . . to be free is not merely to cast off one's chains, but to live in a way that respects and enhances the freedom of others."[7]

Christ's New Order

To be human is not about looking for wisdom, beauty or strength in someone; nor is it about deep faith, good works and prayer. For us as Christians, it is more about recognizing the face of God in others, seeing them as fellow human beings created by God and of worth for that very reason. In Psalm 8 we read this about human beings: "You have made them a little lower than the angels and crowned them with glory and honour" (Ps 8:5). It doesn't matter if a person has a severe learning disability: he or she is still valued by God, created by him, and is crowned with glory and honour. What an amazing truth! Frequently, for the person living with disability, the lack of acceptance by others leads to self-hatred. How can you learn to love yourself when those around you treat you as if you have no ability, cannot be independent, and are worth little in the eyes of the world? God's world is different; and we, as Christ's followers, are examples of the new order: that of the weak being strong (1 Cor 1:27–29), the rejected being chosen (Mark 10:31; Luke 13:30), the poor in spirit becoming rich in God's understanding (Matt 5:3) and the blind having insight (John 9:25–33). God believes in us, chose us and has plans for us – plans to build us up and to give us a hope and a future (Jer 29:11).

Summary

To fully discuss what it means to be human would take an entire book, but we have briefly engaged with the question and considered some key aspects. We have seen that every person's foundational relationship is with God himself, and therefore, when we connect with one another, we are connecting with God in the other person, which should surely encourage an attitude of mutual respect. We affirm that all human beings need to be loved and valued in order to flourish, and that a sense of belonging in relationship with others brings mutual healing. When inclusion and integration into society becomes the norm, we share the freedom to be the people God created us to be.

---

7. Nelson Mandela, *Long Walk to Freedom* (Boston: Little, Brown and Company, 1995), 751.

12

One Body: Sharing Our Gifts

Just as the body, though one, has many parts, but all its many parts form one body, so it is with Christ. (1 Cor 12:12)

The Body: A Unified Entity

The body is amazing, isn't it? There are so many parts to it, all with different jobs to do to keep us healthy, but they all depend on one another to function properly. There is no part of the body that is not important if we desire wholeness.

It's the same with the church, which is often called "the body of Christ." This body also has many members, each with a part to play in fulfilling the Great Commission of Matthew 28:19–20. If some members of the body of Christ are denied their part to play, the unity and wholeness of the body of Christ is threatened.

Paul is very clear about unity in the words he uses when he describes the body: "For we were all baptised by one spirit so as to form one body – whether Jews or Gentiles, slave or free – and we were all given the one spirit to drink. And so the body is not made up of one part but of many" (1 Cor 12:13–14).

If we try to place ourselves into the position of those who first heard these words of Paul, we will begin to understand how alarming his statement must have been. Paul claims that whether we are Jews or Gentiles, we are one in unity through the Spirit. The Jews often believed that Gentiles were unclean, so talk of equality with the Gentiles was difficult for them to accept. We know how important tribal affiliation can be; it can be a part of who we are, our identity. Paul claims that despite these differences we are drawn into a unity through the Holy Spirit that is stronger and more fundamental than the differences, and this unity overrules all else. The indwelling of the Holy Spirit enables us to respect one another's differences and to creatively use those differences so our gifts are revealed in the body of Christ.

Unity Includes and Values Others

But our differences are not only in respect of our being Jew or Gentile, or of belonging to one particular tribe or another: we can include the difference between living with disability and being able-bodied. If Paul is talking of one body of Christ through the Spirit, surely this unity includes people with disability? The truth is, though, that as a church we frequently forget the gifts people with disability can bring to the body of Christ; we forget that unity through the Spirit is more fundamental than being able-bodied or disabled.

Paul uses an amusing story to illustrate his point regarding valuing one another's gifts. We could retell the story this way:

> One day, the foot was feeling really cross because he felt that nobody treated him well. He decided that he would complain to the body, so he said: "I want to be a hand. The hand is important; everybody likes the hand and cares for it because it does intricate things. If I am not a hand, then I don't feel I belong to the body."
>
> Then the ear heard his complaint and thought, "Now is my chance to complain"; so he joined in by saying: "Well, I'm not important either; everyone thinks the eye is important because it is on the front of the face. I am stuck on the side of the head, so no one cares about me! The eye is part of the body, but I'm not a part of the body."
>
> There was a short silence, and then God said, "I made the body. Every single part of the body is important and has a job to do. Even the parts that people think are not important I make especially important."
>
> After that everyone was happy because each part felt respected and had a job to do in the body. (See 1 Cor 12:15–20.)

Behind an amusing story there is often truth that needs to be absorbed. Do people with disability ever feel helpless and hopeless when trying to use their gifts in the church? As we discussed in the previous chapter, to be valued is an important part of being human, and it nurtures self-confidence and maturity. In Paul's illustration, the parts of the body begin to quarrel because they are not looking at each other's gifts, but at how important each individual part feels in the body. People with disability worship the same God as those without disability, are baptized by the same Holy Spirit and are given gifts for use in the body of Christ, but they are often denied the opportunity to use those gifts. Dachollom Datiri comments, "The different parts of a body all need each other, just as individual Christians need one another. This point is well made by the African proverb, 'The left hand washes the right and the right hand washes the left.'"[1]

Valuing One Another's Gifts

We have already noted how each part of the physical body works in relationship with other parts of the body. In the church, we can encourage an attitude of valuing each person's contribution to the fellowship and mission of the church, whether they have a disability or not. This attitude says, "You have gifts that we can use in our fellowship." We will look at this in more detail in chapter 20. "If we spot what skills people have and give them encouragement and support to use their God-given gifts, people gain a reputation for doing what they're good at. Too often, however, people are criticised and pulled down, made to feel embarrassed or ashamed."[2]

In Ephesians, Paul writes the following words: "For we are God's handiwork, created in Christ Jesus to do good works, which God prepared in advance for us to do" (Eph 2:10). Who are the "we" Paul is talking about? It is we human beings, created in the image of God; we are transformed by his grace, bearing his image, and with a desire to do his work here on earth. That deep desire and passion to do God's work is not limited to those who are able-bodied; for every one of us, a work has been planned.

This is a challenging thought! Perhaps you have a picture in your mind of a person who seems to have little understanding of the world around. You might wonder, "How can that person have a part to play in our church?" This is a valid question and one we should not avoid. We might need to ask another question: Is it necessary that good works are active, or can they be passive? Let's look at this more closely; we'll use a short story as an illustration.

Rachel had returned from a really hard day of work; she was feeling tired and upset by the attitude of her boss. "I don't feel like cooking the tea for Mother," she thought. "I would rather spend the evening watching something on the TV. But I know Mother is tired from looking after Michael all day, so I suppose I shall have to cook." Not for the first time, Rachel felt annoyed that her older brother, who had severe learning difficulties, took up so much precious family time. In a bad mood, Rachel went through to where her brother was sitting in his wheelchair. "Hi, Michael," she greeted him. "Are you OK?"

---

1. Dachollom Datiri, in *Africa Bible Commentary*, ed. Tokunboh Adeyemo (Nairobi: Word Alive; Grand Rapids, MI: Zondervan, 2006), 1392.

2. Tony Phelps-Jones, *Making Church Accessible to All: Including Disabled People in Church Life* (Abingdon: Bible Reading Fellowship, 2013), 138.

Michael slowly turned his head towards her and looked at her with quiet, untroubled eyes and a faint smile. There was a profound peace about him which Rachel suddenly recognized was far stronger than her agitation and frustration. It almost seemed as if Michael had been filled with that "peace that passes understanding." As her brother continued to look at her with patience and trust, Rachel slowly felt her troubles melt away. "Oh, Lord, I think you've just spoken to me about peace and contentment," she whispered. "Thank you for the reminder." She set about preparing the meal, but now she felt much more relaxed, and was very thankful to God for encouraging her through Michael.

Michael hadn't *done* anything; he was just himself, created, loved and used by God to bless others. His trust in Rachel was an example of what our trust in Christ should be.

If we truly believe that each person is uniquely God's workmanship, then what is written in 1 Corinthians 12:7 will become evident: "Now to each one the manifestation of the Spirit is given for the common good." Dachollom Datiri comments, "As always, he [Paul] stresses that everyone has a gift that is very useful in the community and that gifts are not given for the benefit of the gifted person, but for the common good."[3]

Including Our Brothers and Sisters with Disability

In some respects, including our brothers and sisters with disability in the life of the church should not be any different from including anyone else. It is a question of discerning their gifts and finding out from them what ministry they feel God may be calling them to be involved with in the church. This might necessitate encouraging them to believe that they do have a gift to share. People with disabilities are often marginalized, and this leads to a lack of self-belief. Inclusion is about setting them free to use their gifts within the body of the church. As we saw in the previous chapter, we lose our own freedom when we deny a person the freedom to use his or her gifts for the church. We should encourage an attitude of developing the abilities of others within the body of Christ. This will be covered in detail in chapter 20.

Perhaps a more challenging question needs to be asked: Is it uncomfortable for "normal" Christians when someone with obvious impairment takes the offertory and limps to the front? Is there reluctance to allow a person with learning impairment and little speech to hand out the books before the service? We need to be very honest with ourselves and identify the barriers that prevent

---

3. Datiri, *Africa Bible Commentary*, 1392.

people with disability from being a visible part of the church. If we do feel uncomfortable, what is the reason for this feeling? Can we accept that maybe we need to change our attitude so that we can see the face of Christ in our brothers and sisters with disability? Myroslaw Tataryn offers this thought:

> What if this church minister presumed that the parishioners with disabilities belonged alongside other parishioners? It would take effort to learn how to accommodate the particularities of the people who seem too different to blend in with the average. It requires creativity. It would certainly necessitate dialogue with each person who needed accommodation. It would compel relationship. It would create sanctuary. In fact, it would be a testament to the example that Jesus presents to his disciples, often to their dismay: speaking to, eating with, noticing, and addressing the very people he was expected to shun.[4]

Summary

Recognizing the gifts of people living with disability and creating an opportunity for them to use their gifts should be a normal part of church life, an acknowledgment of the church being one body. Sadly, some parts of the body are denied their rightful active place within the church, and find themselves as marginalized there as they are in everyday life. But is it not true to say that a church that does not include people living with disability is an incomplete church?

---

4. Myroslaw Tataryn and Maria Truchan-Tataryn, *Discovering Trinity in Disability* (New York: Orbis, 2013), 17.

Section III

Welcome to Our Inclusive Church!

Introduction to Section III

Section III offers practical application for church leaders and the community regarding disability. The ideas are based on an African context. Chapter 15 highlights some basic human rights in relation to disability. The rights of people with disabilities have been denied not only in families but also in society generally. This chapter looks at a few Articles of the UN Convention on the Rights of Persons with Disabilities. The intention is to awaken readers to recognize people with disabilities as participatory members of society who have rights just like other people. It also encourages church and community leaders to set an example in the protection of the rights of people with disabilities.

Chapter 16 investigates whether there is equality of opportunities for women and men with disabilities. In an African context the level of marginalization between women and men with disabilities varies. In most African countries women with disabilities experience more discrimination than men due to persistent beliefs that cause double discrimination on the basis of their being both a woman and disabled. Such women not only have limited participation in society, but are also exposed to sexual abuse and other forms of physical violence that can threaten their lives. Social barriers deepen the vulnerability of these women to remaining voiceless even if they experience their rights being denied or violated. This chapter highlights that everybody has a role to play in working towards the equality of women and men with disabilities. We will also learn that to bring about gender equality, the journey should start as early as possible, immediately from childhood. This should be done practically, from family level to community level. Community leaders, including church leaders, should effect change by sensitizing the community regarding gender equality and by providing opportunities for both women and men with disabilities at various levels of leadership.

In chapter 17 we look at the relationship between disability and poverty, and how they affect each other. We will see how people with disabilities, especially in Africa, face limited social and economic opportunities that ultimately lead them into poverty. People with disability are often led to believe that their condition cannot be treated in the hospital, so they depend on traditional medicines; this leads to a deterioration in their situation and increases their poverty. Poor people are at higher risk of inadequate nutrition and inability to access health interventions; this can either worsen an existing disability or cause disability to occur in the first place. This chapter will demonstrate that both the poor and the rich, whether disabled or not, live in the same community. The question is how those who have much can support those with disability who have little in order to improve their livelihoods. We acknowledge that some organizations, including church organizations, have contributed to the efforts of governments in dealing with social challenges. However, it is not clear whether the services that are offered benefit both disabled and non-disabled equally. We also see that some people, due to their disability, lack the confidence to lead meaningful lives. The church can help by encouraging them to understand their condition and realize their potential, and by empowering them to actively participate in development activities.

In chapter 18 we will see why advocacy is important for people with disabilities. People with disabilities in African society do not enjoy the same level of access to their rights as people without disability. This proves the necessity of advocacy work for people with disabilities. We should acknowledge that advocating for people with disabilities is not easy; it needs commitment and patience, because it normally takes time to realize the results of advocacy work. Advocacy can be frustrating because it is complex and sometimes touches people's personal interests; therefore, it is important to overcome barriers and learn from challenges. This chapter looks at the necessary skills and how to put advocacy into practice, remembering that advocacy can be more effective when people with disabilities speak for themselves, because they know the challenges they face better than anyone else. Have you ever thought that Jesus engaged in advocacy? This chapter shows that the Bible clearly justifies the role of someone speaking on behalf of others.

Inclusion of people with disabilities in all areas of life is becoming a more critical issue in society. The final chapters identify some practical questions to discuss. For example, is your church a disability-inclusive church? These chapters suggest ideas for creating a church that is accessible and inclusive. A physical environment that is friendly to people with disability is the first thing to consider when constructing a church or making adjustments. People with limited mobility need adjusted infrastructure to meet their needs. Chapter 20 includes ideas for making the church physically accessible, in particular, creating ramps and accessible toilets. When deciding to make your church accessible, you need also to think about creating an inclusive service. Do not think only about people with physical disabilities; people with visual, hearing and intellectual impairment, for example, all have particular needs in order to participate in the service.

We all agree that we are created with different abilities, but it is important to recognize the different talents and gifts of each person irrespective of his or her condition. Everyone has something to offer in the church when we are all given the opportunity to participate.

13

Disability and Human Rights: Not Just a Secular Issue

The whole area of "rights" can be controversial, especially when we add in the variety of views that come from people of different denominations, faiths and even political backgrounds. In this chapter we will look briefly at some basic human rights, and then consider a few elements of the United Nations Convention on the Rights of Persons with Disabilities.

Part of our work as a community-based programme is to make home visits to families with children with a disability. Sometimes we notice a contrast between the clothing of the child with a disability and that of his or her siblings; the child with a disability might be wearing threadbare clothes, perhaps torn and providing little warmth, while the siblings are better dressed. The parents might explain that it is difficult to clothe all the children in the same way. While it is understandable that the financial challenges of keeping a family clothed, fed and educated are immense, this situation raises certain questions. Is a value judgment being made about the child with disability? Why was that child not clothed adequately, so that he/she felt cold, while the others wore adequate clothing? Perhaps the child was not valued equally with other children in the family. The child with disability is more dependent on the care-giver; but the extra time and attention required may be withdrawn, leaving the child without good hygiene.

Jesus taught a different way in Matthew 25:31–40. Although this is a well-known text, it contains a message that we can miss through familiarity: when someone takes the time or makes the sacrifice to respect those who others consider to be less worthy, that person is, in fact, showing respect and commitment to God.

What Are Basic Human Rights?

The Equality and Human Rights Commission states, "Human rights are the basic rights and freedoms that belong to every person in the world, from birth until death. . . . These basic rights are based on shared values like dignity, fairness, equality, respect and independence. These values are defined and protected by law."[1]

In the UN Universal Declaration of Human Rights, many of the Articles are concerned with freedom from attitudes and actions that seek to diminish or harm a person, and freedom to live in a manner that respects difference, including that of age, gender and physical and mental ability. Article 25 states, "Everyone has the right to a standard of living adequate for the health and well-being of himself and of his family, including food, clothing, housing and medical care and necessary social services . . ."[2]

Although the universal respect for human rights is far from being a reality, we should all be working towards this, and church leaders can encourage this in their contact with community leaders. Perhaps the human rights we talk about are the very things that Jesus was teaching and demonstrating throughout his life.

A Special Declaration for Persons with Disabilities

In December 2006 a new Convention was adopted which focused on people living with disability; this was called the UN Convention on the Rights of Persons with Disabilities. It became active in May 2008. The need for this new Convention arose from the negative experiences that people with disabilities continually faced in society, often being denied the basic human rights of an equal standard of living and equality of opportunity with those who did not have a disability. It brought about a change from the view that people with disabilities are objects to be pitied and cared for, to recognizing them as participatory members of society who have the right to make decisions about their lives and to take responsibilities like other people. Part of the opening Article states, "The purpose of the present Convention is to promote, protect and ensure the full enjoyment of all human rights and fundamental

---

1. "What Are Human Rights?," Equality and Human Rights Commission, accessed 29 October 2018, https://www.equalityhumanrights.com/en/human-rights/what-are-human-rights.

2. "Universal Declaration of Human Rights," United Nations, accessed 29 October 2018, http://www.un.org/en/universal-declaration-human-rights/.

freedoms by all persons with disabilities, and to promote respect for their inherent dignity."[3]

It is not possible to look at every Article of the Convention here, but a few are worthy of special attention. Article 9 states, "To enable persons with disabilities to live independently and participate fully in all aspects of life, States Parties shall take appropriate measures to ensure to persons with disabilities access, on an equal basis with others, to the physical environment, to transportation, to information and communications . . ."[4] It was observed in one East African country that wheelchair users travelling on public transport are charged to put their wheelchair on the luggage carrier. This doubles the fare, which for someone who may already be living at or near poverty level makes travelling very expensive. The result is that the person becomes housebound, rarely socializing with others. The wheelchair acts as the person's legs, and under Article 9 such a person has a right to access all aspects of society.

Article 3 states:

> The principles of the present Convention shall be:
>
> 1. Respect for inherent dignity, individual autonomy including the freedom to make one's own choices, and independence of persons;
>
> 2. Non-discrimination;
>
> 3. Full and effective participation and inclusion in society;
>
> 4. Respect for difference and acceptance of persons with disabilities as part of human diversity and humanity;
>
> 5. Equality of opportunity;
>
> 6. Accessibility;
>
> 7. Equality between men and women;
>
> 8. Respect for the evolving capacities of children with disabilities and respect for the right of children with disabilities to preserve their identities.[5]

---

3. "Article 1," Convention on the Rights of Persons with Disabilities, United Nations, accessed 1 November 2018, https://www.un.org/development/desa/disabilities/convention-on-the-rights-of-persons-with-disabilities/article-1-purpose.html.

4. "Article 9: Accessibility," Convention on the Rights of Persons with Disabilities, United Nations, accessed 1 November 2018, https://www.un.org/development/desa/disabilities/convention-on-the-rights-of-persons-with-disabilities/article-9-accessibility.html.

5. "Article 3: General Principles," Convention on the Rights of Persons with Disabilities, accessed 1 November 2018, https://www.un.org/development/desa/disabilities/convention-on-the-rights-of-persons-with-disabilities/article-3-general-principles.html.

This Article includes participation and inclusion as a part of human rights. Although in some countries there is improvement at government level with regard to this, many countries still fail to allow people with disability to actively participate in society and decision-making. In those countries where improvement has taken place, the church has played a role in leading the way. As a church leader, are you prepared to take up this challenge? In his life, Jesus was an example of inclusion, always noticing and caring for the marginalized and forgotten members of society. Examples of this are found in Mark 1:40–42; 5:24b–34; Luke 13:10–17; 17:11–19.

Sections Regarding Education and Health

Article 24 highlights the right of children to education on an equal basis with others, while Article 25 talks of equal access to health facilities and treatment. Are we close to achieving equality of education and health care? Some countries have put in place policies regarding inclusive education, but implementation remains a big challenge.

Figure 13.1. Pupils at a special unit with their teacher.
Photo ©Bridget Hathaway.

Many governments have limited resources, and they may prioritize other development issues. Concerning health care, people with disability still experience prejudice when they visit health facilities. For example, people on epilepsy medication need to visit their health centre every month to receive it. It is not uncommon for a person with a disability to sit all day waiting to be seen by the health assistant, while others arrive, receive treatment and leave. Is this not discrimination?

It is worthwhile reading the summary of the UN Convention on the Rights of Persons with Disabilities, which can be found online at the United Nations website at www.un.org/development/desa/disabilities/convention-on-the-rights-of-persons-with-disabilities/the-convention-in-brief.html.

Summary

Richard Lewis says,

> "God chose what is foolish in the world to shame the wise; God chose what is weak to shame the strong. God chose what is low and despised in the world, even things that are not, to bring to nothing things that are" (1 Corinthians 1:27–28). The church ought to be, and often is, an amazing environment for those deemed by society to be the lowest and most unworthy. These were the very people who Jesus chose to be His disciples, for Jesus came to serve, and not be served.[6]

Although the subject of human rights can be complex, we still have a responsibility to act when we see injustice taking place regarding someone with disability. We should seek God's guidance and wisdom, remembering the example of Jesus.

---

6. Richard Lewis, "Disabling Dated Perceptions," Evangelical Alliance, 26 October 2018, https://www.eauk.org/news-and-views/disabling-dated-perceptions.

14

Gender and Disability: Is There Equality of Opportunity?

Gender, and the bringing about of equality between women and men, is a cross-cutting issue all over the world in the development arena. Gender issues address relationships between men and women and their equality of access to, and control of, social resources. In this chapter we look not only at the relationship between gender and disability, but also at equal access for men and women with disabilities to social services and the public responsiveness to their needs.

Aspects of Gender and Disability: Are Women More at Risk of Discrimination Than Men?

In Majority World countries all people with disabilities live in precarious circumstances, but men and women face different challenges. This differs from one society to another. For example, in most African countries, women may experience more discrimination than men due to society's beliefs about woman who have disability. The society may think that women with disabilities are unable to fulfil women's responsibilities, which are seen as having sex and caring for children. In contrast, the society will believe that a man with a disability deserves social opportunities and that he can marry a woman without disability to support him. Women who do not have disabilities themselves are also expected to bear the greater burden of caring for children with disabilities.

In African countries women with disabilities face limitations and greater challenges regarding social participation, particularly with regard to their marriage prospects and possessing resources. Women are also at higher risk of sexual abuse and other forms of physical violence, which endangers their survival. For example, women with disabilities have been raped and left with the burden of caring for children whose fathers are totally absent and often strangers. "There is a strong consensus regarding the risk that both children and women face. 'Women with disabilities are especially vulnerable to discrimination and violence (three to five times more likely to suffer from violence and abuse than the average [female] population).'"[1]

Young women and girls with disabilities are also at higher risk of sexually transmitted diseases due to existing myths in African societies that if you have sex with a girl with disabilities, you will be successful in life and any incurable diseases you have will go away (see chapter 6). What actually happens is that the women with disability become infected with these sexually transmitted diseases. "A recent meta-analysis on the HIV prevalence among adults with disabilities in Sub-Sahara Africa . . . suggests that women with disabilities are especially affected by the HIV epidemic."[2]

Sadly, women with disabilities who face sexual abuse and other forms of physical violence remain silent due to social barriers that limit their ability to seek attention from legal authorities. Due to discrimination, women with disabilities are partially, if not totally, uninvolved in decision-making, even concerning the issues that affect their lives, as cited by the International Disability Alliance: "Women with disabilities represent one in five women worldwide and 65% of the billion people with disabilities across the world. Yet, their voices remain quite silent in mainstream, gender and disability decision-making processes, as well as the gender- or disability- programming often [lacking] to address their rights and needs."[3]

The livelihood status of people with disabilities and those without disabilities is biased in favour of the latter. In Africa, the situation is even worse for women with disabilities because of the inaccessibility for them of educational opportunities compared to men with disabilities. "Women and children face the most discrimination within the disabled community. A report presented to the U.N. Secretary-General on the situation of women and girls

---

1. Carmen Arroyo and Emily Thampoe, quoting André Félix, external communications officer at the European Disability Forum, "Africa: Children and Women with Disabilities, More Likely to Face Discrimination," All Africa, accessed 16 November 2018, https://allafrica.com/stories/201808160405.html.

2. Von Muriel Mac-Seing and Dorothy Boggs, "Triple Discrimination against Women and Girls with Disability," accessed 16 November 2018, https://www.medicusmundi.ch/fr/bulletin/mms-bulletin/adresser-violence-sexuelle-et-vih/adresser-la-violence-sexuelle-et-sexiste-dans-les-projets/triple-discrimination-against-women-and-girls-with-disability.

3. "Participation of Women with Disabilities in Decision-Making Processes," International Disability Alliance, accessed 29 November 2018, http://www.internationaldisabilityalliance.org/events/participation-women-disabilities-decision-making-processes#_ftn1.

with disabilities stated that while 12 percent of men present a disability, a slightly higher amount of women – 19 percent – have a disability. In addition, girls are much less likely to finish primary school than boys, if both present disabilities. And girls are more vulnerable to sexual violence."[4]

Are Women with Disability Disempowered by Society?

Certain cultural practices also jeopardize the ability of women with disabilities to engage in social, political and economic activities. This automatically leaves women with disabilities lagging behind in most aspects of life. Due to inadequate education and lack of exposure to society, women with disabilities remain voiceless, unprotected and unable to enjoy opportunities such as loans offered by the government or other financial institutions which are aimed at raising the financial capacities of individuals. Girls with disabilities are unlikely to attend vocational training where they could acquire vocational skills and probably support themselves.

As discussed in previous chapters, education for children with disabilities in Africa is still inadequate. Children with disabilities in urban areas benefit the most from the few opportunities available. Due to this scarcity of educational opportunities and other issues pertaining to cultural behaviours and beliefs among communities, boys with disabilities have, in general, been given more opportunities than girls. Even those few girls with disabilities who do go to school have a narrow opportunity to attend beyond primary level. For all these reasons, some women with disabilities are forced to go out onto the streets and depend on begging.

Church, Gender and Disability

The general role of the church is to bring people together regardless of their condition because we believe that every person is created in the image of God. Church leaders have good opportunities and influence to work towards equality not only between men and women with disabilities but also between those with and those without disabilities. In order to achieve gender equality, the journey should begin as early as possible from childhood. Children must start seeing women and men, whether disabled or not, carrying out the same roles and responsibilities in the church. In this context, people with disabilities, irrespective of their gender, should be considered for different positions in

---

4. Arroyo and Thampoe, "Africa: Children and Women with Disabilities."

the church in order to promote gender equality and inclusiveness. Church leaders should insist on interaction between able-bodied people and men and women with disabilities. Women with disabilities should be encouraged to accept themselves and be helped and supported to realize their potential and fit into the church community.

We have seen churches that have started disability ministries, which can be very helpful in effecting change in the society. For example, in some countries, the Anglican and Roman Catholic Churches have created disability programmes that reach out to the community. Church leaders are encouraged to speak out on behalf of women with disabilities to ensure the protection of their rights. Sensitization programmes can be included among church activities to lift up women with disabilities to an assured level where they can enjoy social services equally with other groups in the community.

Summary

People with disabilities are denied their human rights in society. The situation for women, however, is often much worse than for men because of their combined womanhood and disability. Discrimination against women with disabilities varies from one society to another – for example, through the denial of education and other social services. When considering gender issues in relation to the church, the role is generally to bring people together without discrimination; to value their abilities, protect their rights, and ensure the equal participation in the church and community of both men and women with disabilities.

15

The Relationship between Poverty and Disability

In an African context, it is impossible to talk about disability without thinking of poverty. In Majority World (low-income) countries, disability and poverty are interlinked; disability can be either a cause or a result of poverty. This is because people with disabilities have limited access to education, health services and other socio-economic opportunities for development. There is a great difference in this respect between what are commonly called "developed" and "developing" countries; in "developed" countries, people with disabilities generally have access to education, health services, and so on. In contrast, in "developing" countries, people with disabilities, who have the same desire to improve their quality of life, have inadequate resources and face social barriers that affect the socio-economic status of themselves and their families.

Can Poverty Cause Disability?

Disability can be a consequence of poverty because people who live below the poverty line are either completely unable or have insufficient resources to meet the basic needs of life. They cannot afford quality health care, which is important for preventing or controlling diseases that can lead to disability. For example, in many parts of Africa, poor people suffer from serious diseases such as osteomyelitis, meningitis, measles, eye diseases and malaria, which require appropriate medical attention. People from poor families delay attending health facilities for proper treatment, and sometimes depend on traditional medicines which may not be helpful. This worsens their condition and can eventually lead to disability.

Poor people also cannot afford healthy food. This leads to malnutrition and lack of nutrients essential for physical and mental development, which may eventually cause disability. Other risks include inadequate public health interventions such as immunization, lack of safe water and sanitation. Inability to afford rehabilitation services such as major surgery or regular medical interventions for long-term physical conditions can either worsen an already present disability or cause another disability. Poverty also increases risks to those living and working in unfair situations that might harm their health.

So Can Disability Cause Poverty?

In many African countries, people with disabilities often face social discrimination or exclusion; this attitude of marginalization propagates their inaccessibility to health care and other social services. People with disabilities are forced to remain in their homes, and this hinders their participation in socio-economic activities within the community. Isolated from the community, such people with disabilities face emotional disturbance, which in turn increases their vulnerability and increases their lack of engagement in economic activities.

Some children with disabilities have no opportunities for education not only because they are not able to go school, but also because they face challenges such as unfriendly infrastructure, inadequate resources and a lack of professionals to help them develop their potential. For this reason, when they grow up they remain unemployed and unable to demonstrate their talents, which could help them to earn a living. Although there are people with disabilities who go to school and get good qualifications, securing work is difficult. This is either because of the inaccessibility of the workplace or persistent social discrimination within the community.

Some people acquire disability in adulthood through serious diseases or accidents. These people will have been providers for their families but suddenly become disabled. They may spend a lot of money and time on treatment and be unable to work, and this leads to a decrease in family income.

Does the Church Have a Role in Alleviating Poverty among People with Disabilities?

The church brings people of different economic classes together to make one family; the rich and the poor worship together and live in the same church community. Some churches have vast resources which are normally contributed by church members, both rich and poor. But how can the church help to improve the livelihoods of its people, especially those with disabilities? We acknowledge that the church (all denominations) has been at the forefront in dealing with social challenges such as hunger, health services and education. But do the services that are offered also benefit people with disabilities to alleviate their poverty? Experience suggests that many churches are focusing on charity support rather than on empowering their people to make a sustainable livelihood. The best way to help people with disabilities and their families is to encourage them to accept and believe that they too are created in the image of God and that they have abilities just like other people, despite their disabling condition (see chapter 9). Help them to realize their potential, and encourage them to utilize their abilities within the church and engage in development activities (see chapter 18).

Try as much as possible to create education opportunities for children and young people with disabilities by advocating for them and linking them with existing schools or vocational centres where they can gain basic knowledge and skills for employment opportunities. The acquired knowledge can help them to start income-generating projects to support themselves. Disability-awareness campaigns led by the church and the entire community could be another way to promote acceptance of people with disabilities. Church leaders can also be responsible in identifying and connecting people with disabilities to disability organizations, where they can access rehabilitation services. This may help alleviate their disabling conditions and open up access to social services that will eventually decrease their vulnerability. The church should lead the way by realizing the abilities that people with disabilities have and by creating employment opportunities within the church.

Summary

Based on what we have discussed in this chapter, we conclude that disability is both a cause and a consequence of poverty. We have seen a strong relationship between the two. The church has a great opportunity to effect change in the community to ensure that people with disabilities can escape from poverty. But the church cannot do it alone, without the involvement of other stakeholders, including people with disabilities themselves. As one big family, the church is in a good position to sensitize the community to ensure the best engagement of people with disabilities in development activities.

16

Advocacy

Part 1: Advocacy from a General Viewpoint

Many people who are engaged in advocacy are probably not aware that this is what they are doing. If a person is involved in any activity that seeks to protect the rights of disadvantaged people or groups, automatically that person is doing advocacy. Advocacy often focuses on bringing changes in social attitudes and unfair public structures that affect the lives of marginalized groups. It can be done by individuals or by groups of people to speak out on behalf of others whose rights have been abused.

Although protecting people's rights should be mandatory for everyone, some people are either ignorant of the issues or are not able to engage in advocacy work because of personal interests. Experience shows that people with disabilities, especially in African countries, are victims of discrimination and social injustice in their communities. Activists have been struggling to speak on their behalf to ensure protection of their rights, but still we notice the continuing violation of their rights, even by their own families. Some governments have come up with good policies that, if put into practice, might positively improve the lives of people with disabilities. Unfortunately, these policies remain unimplemented; in this case it is not just ignorance or negligence, but also a lack of political will, that contributes to this situation.

Is Advocacy Really Needed for People with Disabilities?

People with disabilities are marginalized and disadvantaged in most societies due to the social challenges they face. These challenges may differ from one society to another. For example, in one society, people with disabilities may have access to education or health care but have limitations in political participation; in another society, they may enjoy other social services but have no opportunity for employment. Therefore, people with disabilities do not enjoy the same level of access to social services compared with able-bodied people. Speaking out on their behalf to bring them at least close to other people's level is therefore very important.

Is It Easy to Do Advocacy for People with Disabilities?

Advocating for the rights of people with disabilities, like other advocacy activities, needs commitment and patience. It usually takes a long time to realize the results of advocacy work. Those who are doing advocacy with and for people with disabilities should be well informed about the existing legal frameworks and government structures responsible for protecting the rights of people with disabilities. The ability to identify and analyse issues is crucial because any issue needs to be analysed critically and communicated to those whom you seek to support.

For example, imagine you witness a parent mistreating his child with a disability, and you want to take action; you must be sure that the mistreatment of the child is not a single act but happens repeatedly, and that it will have a harmful impact on the child. You would also need to think of other people who can support you in protecting the rights of that child. How do other family members feel about that problem, or are they also part of the problem? Are they able to help the parent to change his behaviour? Do you know what the law says about that problem? If the parent fails to agree with your advice and counselling, are you able to petition people in power to work on the problem with you and bring justice in the situation? You will need to be careful when doing advocacy because sometimes it creates a conflict between you and the person you are dealing with. Providing clear information to the family to help them understand the problem is very important, because sometimes people do things because of ignorance.

Is It Possible for Advocacy to Be Done by One Person?

It is possible to do advocacy alone, especially when the issue you are advocating about involves just one person or one family. This normally requires awareness sessions and counselling to the individual or family. Creating awareness and counselling can be done by one person who is able to identify the problem, analyse it and then act as an agent of change for the individual, family or group. This is mostly done by professionals such as social workers, community workers, lawyers and other people with ability to carry the problems of others and feel part of them. People with disabilities can also speak out to represent the ideas of others either to the government or other authorities, so long as they have the ability to communicate information and convince other people to understand and agree on the issue.

Advocacy can also be done by an organized group of people; this could be community groups or disabled persons associations (DPAs). This can be more effective because people with disabilities can then speak for themselves. These groups may sometimes need guidance from professionals or someone from the group who has advocacy skills. They should know the message they want to communicate, who to approach and the appropriate time to meet with that particular person. It is especially important to use groups for advocacy when the issue you are advocating about affects policies or common social practices. Groups can use public campaigns or media to raise awareness to effect changes in the community.

Figure 16.1. Community meetings can be a powerful tool in advocacy.
Photo ©Julieth Aloyce. Used by permission.

Stakeholders' Involvement in Advocacy Work

The involvement of other stakeholders in advocacy is inevitable. The nature of the issue you intend to advocate about will determine which people you need to engage with. Identifying relevant stakeholders is an important step, especially when you are dealing with an issue that affects a majority of people.

You might decide to have a get-together event or a meeting where you table your subject for discussion; through that meeting you will find supporters, but also people who will not be able to support you. Start by engaging with those who support your idea; slowly you can succeed in convincing those who were reluctant. A clear plan will guide you on what you want to achieve and the steps to take towards the intended achievement.

This approach is mainly applied in advocacy work aimed at changing general systems or practices in the community. Advocacy for individuals may not need systematic planning; rather, you will need a good understanding of the problem, what you want to inform the individual and the approach you will use.

Challenges in Doing Advocacy

When doing advocacy, especially in public, a number of people will be involved, not all of whom will be on your side. Others may wish you to fail, and maybe very few – or even nobody at all – will support you. This can be even worse when you accuse influential people or government officials of not upholding the rights of people with disability. Sometimes you will seem foolish in the eyes of others; this might cause you to step back and end up unsuccessful. In this situation, you need to be courageous and continue moving forward. The most important thing is to ensure that you have the facts for what you are speaking about. Try as much as possible to share clear information with people to make them aware of the issue and convince them to be at your side. If you are using a campaign, make sure you mobilize people and have the assurance of a large number of supporters during the campaign. Identify potential people who could help you to influence others or who could push things forward. If you succeed by getting even a few people on your side, use that advantage to help you predict obstacles you might face, and ask them to assist in setting out strategies on how you can avoid or overcome the obstacles.

Summary

You may feel disappointed when you do advocacy for the first time and things do not work out. It needs patience and courage because advocacy involves working on and changing the minds of people. It is a time-consuming work because realizing achievements can be slow; but the achievements of advocacy work are worth celebrating. How wonderful it is to make the voice of the voiceless heard and to let them feel like other people in the community!

Part 2: Advocacy from a Theological Viewpoint

Advocacy and human rights are closely linked, as we discussed in chapter 15. Often, we are advocating with or on behalf of people with disability because those human rights are being abused. For example, a young woman with disability might be raped and the offender escapes punishment. That woman's right to justice has been abused.

Advocacy is not a secular concept; far from it. Jesus spent time challenging the unjust ways of the ruling authorities and those in power in the synagogues. In the Old Testament there are many laws that are founded on compassion and justice, and instruction by the prophets regarding living out the teaching of the law.

What Does the Bible Say?

In Proverbs we read, "Speak up for those who cannot speak for themselves, for the rights of all who are destitute. Speak up and judge fairly; defend the rights of the poor and needy" (Prov 31:8–9). If we as Christians are people of compassion, that compassion should motivate us to pursue justice for all those who, for one reason or another, are marginalized. Perhaps you wonder why we should take time to do this when the church's task is to preach the gospel. But has Christ not had compassion on us? By his grace and mercy he has brought us from darkness to light, forgiving confessed sin so that we might be free to be compassionate and merciful towards others.

Micah speaks out clearly the words of the Lord: "He [the LORD] has shown you, O mortal, what is good. And what does the LORD require of you? To act justly and to love mercy and to walk humbly with your God" (Mic 6:8). In this verse we are actually told that God *requires* us to act justly and be merciful; it is not a choice but a requirement for Christians. Perhaps we will only feel that deep desire to help others and be compassionate when we ourselves are humble before God, acknowledging his great sacrifice for us.

God's "Ordinary" People Are Involved in Advocacy

Jesus persistently advocated on behalf of people with a variety of needs. He healed a crippled woman on the Sabbath, challenging the law that would have kept her disabled and impoverished (Luke 13:10–17). We read of a similar action in John 5:1–15, and in Matthew 23:23–24 Jesus is outspoken: "Woe to you, teachers of the law and Pharisees, you hypocrites! You give a tenth of your spices – mint, dill and cumin. But you have neglected the more important matters of the law – justice, mercy and faithfulness" (Matt 23:23a).

However, it was not just Jesus who took up the role of being an advocate on behalf of those who had no power; we read of many others who did the same. "Over and over in Scripture, God sends ordinary men and women, from a variety of sources, to speak to the most powerful leaders of the day and express his displeasure with the ruling perpetrators of injustice. Moses, Nathan, Esther, Paul and others all obeyed God's call to speak for those in need. Similarly, God's call to us is to bridge the gap between our leaders and those who have no voice."[1]

Imagine how the Israelites felt when they were enslaved in Egypt; they were a people who had no power themselves to gain justice and be heard by the authorities. But God heard their lament: "The LORD said, 'I have indeed seen the misery of my people in Egypt. I have heard them crying out because of their slave drivers, and I am concerned about their suffering. So I have come down to rescue them from the hand of the Egyptians and to bring them up out of that land into a good and spacious land, a land flowing with milk and honey . . .'" (Exod 3:7–8a).

God was concerned about their suffering, but his concern turned into action when he brought the plagues on the Egyptians, resulting in the freedom of his captive people. His concern and compassion were accompanied by action. However, God used Moses and Aaron as his team of advocates; weak and imperfect human beings were chosen by God to speak on his behalf. This should encourage us as we seek to follow God's calling to speak against injustice and to bring life in all its fullness to people living with disability.

How Can the Church Be Involved in Advocacy?

The mission of the church is to bring the good news of the gospel to all people, whatever their background. What is this good news? Surely it is summarized in John 3:16: "For God so loved the world that he gave his one and only Son, that whoever believes in him shall not perish but have eternal life."

Our broken relationship with God is restored through Jesus – through his death and resurrection. This restoration to God's plan for his world is not just for us as individuals but for all humankind. When we speak out on behalf of

---

1. "Introduction" to International Justice Mission, "Advocacy Devotional: Stand in the Gap," accessed 14 November 2018, https://www.ijmuk.org/documents/Advocacy-Devotional.pdf.

those who have been made vulnerable by society or are marginalized, we are bringing the kingdom of God nearer to them. How do we do this?

We need to examine ourselves and ask if we are really ready for this:

- Do we, as a church, model equality of opportunity, compassion and a heart for serving others?
- Do our sermons and teaching ever touch the subjects of justice, reconciliation and restoration of hope?
- Is the generous use of time on behalf of others seen as part of giving thanks to God for all he has given us? In some churches, giving to God is seen in purely financial terms, but there is more than one way to show our appreciation to God.
- Are we prepared to take up the cause of people who are not respected by society, despite what others might think of us?

These are tough questions, but before you begin advocating with and on behalf of others you must be prepared. Reading about advocacy or inviting someone who has experience in this field to speak on the subject will give you confidence.

Be Careful When You Are Doing Advocacy

Sometimes there is a risk that a particular situation might become political, but as far as possible it is advisable to remain politically neutral; Jesus worked within the laws of the land. However, if what is happening clearly goes against the teaching of Jesus, we have a responsibility to speak out against the breaking of God's law. In some countries, speaking out may put our church members in danger; in this case, great wisdom and diplomacy is needed. Confidentiality is also important; some things can be shared with small groups for prayer, but other things must remain confidential between you and the person concerned. Respect that person by asking for permission before you share anything for prayer.

Summary

Advocating with and on behalf of those who are marginalized is a part of living the Christian life. We may not all be called to be advocates, those who speak out publicly, but we all have a responsibility to take the cause of those who are treated unjustly to someone who can be their advocate. In addition, we can all pray for those who are speaking out, as well as for those who are decision-makers in society. Jeremiah writes, "This is what the LORD says: do what is just and right. Rescue from the hand of the oppressor the one who has been robbed. Do no wrong or violence to the foreigner, the fatherless or the widow, and do not shed innocent blood in this place" (Jer 22:3).

17

Is Your Church a Disability-Inclusive Church?

The concept of inclusion has become very popular in today's culture. This is connected partly with the increasing demand for rights and with minority groups having a stronger voice in some countries. However, the word "inclusion" covers a broad spectrum of situations, so we need to qualify its meaning when we use it in connection with the church.

According to the *Oxford English Dictionary*, "inclusivity" is "The practice or policy of including people who might otherwise be excluded or marginalized, such as those who have physical or mental disabilities and members of minority groups."[1] There are many different types of minority groups, but when we talk about inclusion in this book we are focusing on people living with any kind of disability, including intellectual impairment, physical disability and mental health issues.

Inclusion: The Theory behind the Practice

We have talked about inclusion throughout this book, and have looked at examples of how Jesus was always inclusive in the way he treated people. He always made time for those who were marginalized and were struggling with disability or health issues. Roy McCloughry writes, "To befriend people who have experienced brokenness is to realise that although at that point their story may differ from ours, they are no different from us. We become more human as we learn from one another, and to do so is to make time for one another."[2]

---

1. "Inclusivity," Oxford Living Dictionaries, accessed 30 October 2018, https://en.oxforddictionaries.com/definition/inclusivity.

2. Roy McCloughry, *The Enabled Life: Christianity in a Disabling World* (London: SPCK, 2013), 2.

The first stage in practising inclusion as a church is to make time for members of your church who are disabled or who have a family member with disability. However many ramps and special seats you might have in your church, if church members continue to exclude those using the ramps and special seats, inclusion has not taken place. To quote Roy McCloughry again: "If I believe that who I am depends on what I have achieved, I am unlikely to value the life of someone with an intellectual impairment. I can live my life without that person. To break this deadlock takes courage"[3]

Our society today tells us that what we own, wear and achieve are the things that give us value. An expensive smartphone is a status symbol, playing football in the school or college team will bring popularity and good exam results will open the way to university. But what happens when none of this is possible? Someone with intellectual impairment achieves little in the eyes of the world; but what about in God's eyes? Does God have gifts for those who understand differently from us?

As we love and respect people with intellectual impairment we will seek the gifts that God has given them to share with us. These gifts may not be what we expect; they maybe an accepting smile or a touch of the hand that ministers to us in a trusting friendship that speaks of God's acceptance given to us through that person.

Sometimes people with intellectual impairment have spiritual insight that is based on simplicity; this can reveal truths to us that we may miss because of our intellectualism. We might achieve great things and be appreciated for what we have accomplished; but do we appreciate the achievements of those with intellectual impairment? They might seem small achievements to us, but they are big successes in their eyes.

> Theological competence is not a prerequisite of saving faith. For that we may be thankful. . . . In sharing in it [the Eucharist] as one of the family, perhaps simply at the level of being included rather than excluded, some who are handicapped may be helped to discern experientially the reality of God's love for them.[4]

When inclusion is talked about, people are more likely to think about physical disabilities than intellectual impairment. McCloughry is right when he says it takes "courage" to change people's perceptions because of the inherent discomfort many people feel when faced with unpredictable responses.

---

3. McCloughry, *Enabled Life*, 2.

4. David A. Pailin, *A Gentle Touch: From a Theology of Handicap to a Theology of Human Being* (London: SPCK, 1992), 144.

However, to be truly inclusive is to realize the worth of every individual in the eyes of God, whether they are "like us" or not. For leaders in the church and wider community, this changed perception will bring challenges; but the strength to face these challenges is found in God's infinitely great love for his creation. Ephesians 3:14–17 says, "For this reason I kneel before the Father, from whom every family in heaven and on earth derives its name. I pray that out of his glorious riches he may strengthen you with power through his Spirit in your inner being, so that Christ may dwell in your hearts through faith."

The power to create a disability-inclusive church will come from God working through his church leaders.

A Case Study

The following true story shows how the church can bring hope to people living without much hope.

It is not unusual for a husband to leave his wife when a child with disability is born; the blame for the disability is frequently placed on the wife and her family. In a certain village two brothers suffered from a progressive disability which rendered them unable to walk. Their father took another wife and built a house next to his original home. He gave no support to his first wife, and she was unable to spend much time growing crops, as she cared for the boys. Gradually the house collapsed, until it was dangerous to live in. After a local volunteer raised awareness of the situation, and community prejudice about disability was overcome, a new house was built for the family, using village volunteer workforce. Subsequently ministers from two local churches of different denominations worked together to assist the family. One congregation supported the family with their physical needs of clothing and basic essentials while the other congregation focused on their spiritual needs. In this way, collaboration across denominations took place. As the apostle Paul writes, "But God has put the body together, giving greater honour to the parts that lacked it, so that there should be no division in the body, but that its parts should have equal concern for each other. If one part suffers, every part suffers with it; if one part is honoured, every part rejoices with it" (1 Cor 12:24b–26).

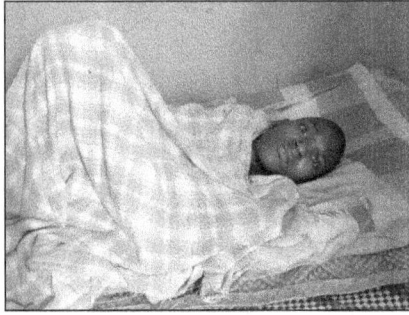

Figure 17.1. One of the brothers safe in his new home.
Photo ©Bridget Hathaway. Used with permission.

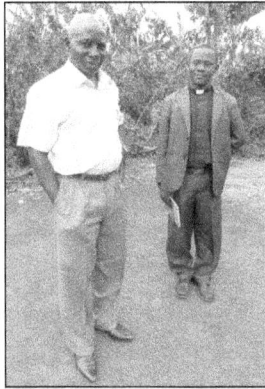

Figure 17.2. The two pastors working together with compassion.
Photo ©Bridget Hathaway. Used with permission.

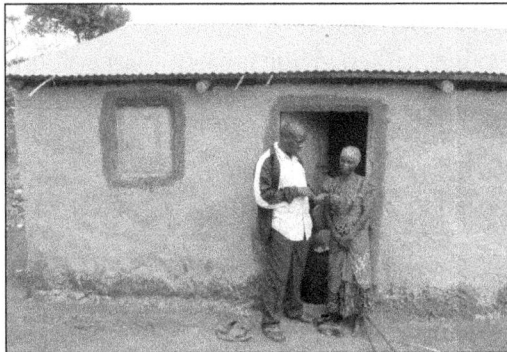

Figure 17.3. The boy's mother outside her new home.
Photo ©Bridget Hathaway. Used with permission.

18

Ideas for Becoming an Accessible and Inclusive Church for People with Disability: Physical Environment

In this chapter we look at practical ways to become an accessible and inclusive church for people with disabilities. It is important that the cost of becoming an accessible church is kept as low as possible. Most churches will struggle to use valuable funds for building such things as ramps or accessible toilets. However, when a wheelchair-user can "wheel" into church instead of crawling in on hands and knees, and can use the toilet, the true value will be realized. Imagine the lack of dignity and self-worth someone feels when they arrive at church wearing nice clothes that then become dirty from having to crawl into the church building. Imagine yourself in that situation, and how it might feel to be crawling at the level of other people's feet.

Ramps

Here are some ideas for making a simple ramp that could be used in your church building.

Points to Note When Making a Ramp

Making a ramp need not be difficult and there is likely to be someone in your community who can help with this task, but there are a number of important points to note.

- The ramp needs to be strong and firm, able to carry the weight of the wheelchair-user, the wheelchair itself and the person assisting the wheelchair-user.
- If the wheelchair-user is independent, a steep ramp will be very difficult for him or her to use. The longer the ramp, the less steep it will be; the shorter the ramp, the steeper it will be.
- The surface of the ramp should not be slippery in any conditions, so a slightly rough surface that will grip both tyres and shoes is essential.
- It is helpful to have low sides to the ramp to prevent the wheelchair rolling off the side, especially when descending the ramp.
- A handrail on one side of the ramp is helpful for those with limited mobility who need extra support when walking.

What Material Can Be Used to Make a Ramp?

A ramp can be made from strong wood, earth or cement.

- If you make it from earth, mix it with grass; the mixture should be compressed until it is solid, almost like cement. As mentioned above, you will need to ensure that the surface is not slippery in rain; using aggregates can help achieve this.
- If you make it from wood, you will need to use a strong dense wood that will not split or break under pressure. Treat the wood with old engine oil or a special wood preserver that will protect it from termites and other wood-destroying insects.
- If you make it from cement, make the surface slightly rough to give a good grip for the tyres of the wheelchair.

Measuring for a Ramp

It can be surprising how much space a ramp will take up! If you make it too short, it will be too steep and will make independent mobility almost impossible. The recommended "rise" for a wheelchair is:

For every 2.54 cm (1 inch) of rise you will need 30.48 cm
(12 inches) of ramp length.

So, for example, if your ramp needs to be 0.6 m (2 feet) high, it will need to be 7.31 m (24 feet) long. This is a 1:12 ratio.[1]

Figure 18.1. A long ramp with the recommended gradient and two handrails. Photo ©Bridget Hathaway.

Figure 18.2. A short ramp near to a wall with a single handrail. Photo ©Bridget Hathaway.

Figure 18.3. Sideview of the ramp showing how it will fit next to steps. Photo ©Bridget Hathaway.

It is possible to make a steeper ramp, but it will be harder to use independently.

---

1. "How to Measure for a Ramp: Wheelchairs & Scooters," Preferred Health Choice, accessed 3 November 2018, https://www.phc-online.com/wheelchair-ramp-chart_a/131.htm.

If your church already has steps built at the front entrance, it should be possible to build a ramp at one of the side entrances. Perhaps one day you will have a pastor who is a wheelchair-user; how will he serve his church if he cannot get inside the building? If members of the congregation object to using money to build a ramp because there are currently no church members who have disabilities or are wheelchair-users, the answer is simple: people with physical disabilities are probably not in church because of the challenges of access. If getting inside the building is a challenge, they are unlikely to feel they are welcome!

Figure 18.4. A short ramp by the side door of a rural church. Photo ©Bridget Hathaway.

Is Your Toilet Accessible for People with Limited Mobility?

You may think that making a toilet seat is just too much trouble. However, you will find that it will help more than just those with disability. There are elderly people who find it hard to use a pit latrine, as their legs become stiff and weak with old age. Jesus was someone who went the "extra mile," and we are asked to do the same.

The following explains designs for two different types of toilet seat.

Style 1

Figure 18.5. An accessible toilet with a movable seat. Photo ©Bridget Hathaway.

This is a simple design in which the seat is placed over the toilet hole. The stool is made from strong wood. It is important to measure carefully so the hole on the stool fits over the hole in the ground. The height of the stool should be the height of an average wheelchair seat, approximately 53 cm from the ground to the seat. When using wood for the toilet seat, it is important to fill any cracks with wood filler. The finished seat should then be varnished with a gloss varnish that is washable. This is to ensure good hygiene.

The picture shows hand bars for the person with disability to hold. The bars can be made from wood, but metal bars will be stronger and will last longer. They do not need to be long, just enough to grip when standing and sitting. They must be very firmly fixed to the wall to avoid accidents which would cause the person to fall. It is important to measure them by using someone who is actually standing and sitting. The lower height should be approximately 74 cm for use when sitting. The higher grip bar could be set at an average person's shoulder height.

Style 2

Figure 18.6. A metal toilet chair. Photo ©Bridget Hathaway.

This is a good design to use if you have several toilets at church and can have a toilet that can be kept for use by those who find it hard to squat, such as older people and people with disability. The chair can be set over the toilet hole and, if possible, near a wall, to reduce the possibility of the chair sliding sideways.

Note: Attention should always be given to hygiene. A bucket of water with a small jug should be kept in the toilet so that the seat can be washed if necessary. Also, the floor under the seat should be rinsed with water after each use.

Summary

Although having a ramp and a special toilet may seem unimportant issues when faced with all the challenges of a parish, making these changes could bring someone into God's kingdom: someone who had thought they were rejected from the family of God because of the physical difficulties of getting into the church building and the lack of accessible facilities there. In Luke 15:5–7, at the end of the parable of the lost sheep, Jesus declares, "I tell you that . . . there will be more rejoicing in heaven over one sinner who repents than over ninety-nine righteous people who do not need to repent" (15:7).

Have you ever thought about the fact that an entire section of society often feels excluded from receiving the good news of the gospel? Right where we are there are people who do not have fellowship because they are unable to access the church building.

19

Ideas for Becoming an Accessible and Inclusive Church for People with Disability: An Inclusive Service

A church service provides a wonderful opportunity to share the gospel message with people, teaching and encouraging them about a Christian lifestyle and sharing God's love with them. However, sometimes a service does not feel welcoming at all; in fact, some people can feel that they should not be there. The welcome at the door might be polite but not welcoming: "Good morning. I am afraid we don't have anywhere for a wheelchair. You will have to sit at the side."

Already the wheelchair-user feels different from others and marginalized. Sitting at the side, in a wheelchair, unable to see clearly when people are standing, all adds to the feeling that he or she is a second-class Christian. But becoming an inclusive and accessible church need not be difficult; it just requires some extra thought and planning.

Here are a few initial suggestions:

- Whenever possible, include the person with disability or his or her family in any planning.
- Try not to make assumptions about the person's ability or needs.
- When possible, imagine yourself in that person's position and try to think what might help you feel like an active member of the church.

Remember that Jesus did not have the attitude that "disabled" means "unable"; Jesus didn't need the concept of "dis-ability" because to him, every person was created to be in the family of God.

Let's Begin at the Door

In the previous chapter we looked at the physical environment, so we can assume that the person with disability has entered the church building. If there is a welcome team, it is a good idea to train them in how to welcome someone who might need guidance. For example, the greeting for a wheelchair-user might be: "Welcome to our church! It is good to see you. Where would you like to sit?"

If your church has chairs, move one chair out of the line, leaving a space so that the wheelchair-user can be part of the row of worshippers. If you use forms or benches in church, slide the form slightly to the left or right (depending on which side the person sits) so the wheelchair-user is on the end of the row but still in line with other people. If you have fixed seating it is more difficult; ask wheelchair-users where they would feel most comfortable sitting.

The greeting for a family with a child with intellectual impairment will be similar, but a little extra reassurance might be needed. For example: "Welcome to our church! It is good to see you. Where would you like to sit? Don't worry if your son becomes restless – you can let him play quietly at the back of church or outside if that would help."

If possible, put a mat on the floor at the back of the church to one side where the child can play; then the care-giver, while remaining with the child, will still be in the church and can participate, to some extent, in the service. Of course, the option to play will depend on the facilities in your church; perhaps there is no space to place a mat at the back of church. If that is the case, the child will have to play outside; there may be no alternative.

The Service of Holy Communion

In many churches, the altar is raised at a higher level from the rest of the church building. In some churches, the worshippers will climb a few steps to kneel near the altar to receive communion. In other churches, the pastor or priest will descend to bring the elements to the people, who will kneel or stand by the steps. For a wheelchair-user or someone with limited mobility, the second option does not create a problem, as the elements are received by the steps. However, if the custom is for communicants to kneel near the altar, you will need to plan the best way to include people with limited mobility.

For a Christian, the service of Holy Communion is a remembrance of Christ's sacrifice on the cross to redeem us from sin. What happens for people who are unable to reach church because of their disability or age? Is their need to receive Holy Communion overlooked? The case study at the end of this chapter shows how a home communion can be organized.

We Are All Different!

If someone sings out of tune or says "Amen" later than everyone else, does it really matter? There is a strong temptation to turn round and see who has the loud voice at the wrong moment, but resist this temptation if you can; allow people to be who God has created them to be, and celebrate the fact that they are in church.

Visual Impairment

Some larger churches produce a weekly newssheet, with prayer points and notices about meetings and activities. It is a good idea to produce a few copies using a larger-size font so that members of the congregation with poor eyesight can keep informed of church activities. Remember also to ensure that pathways are left clear so that a person with visual impairment will not knock in to items left lying around.

Hearing Impairment

For those who have hearing impairment, the ideal situation would be to have someone interpreting a service into sign language, but this is rarely possible. Ensure that people with hearing impairment can sit close to the front where they can both see and hear (if the person has some ability to hear). In this way the person can lip read or listen, whichever suits him or her best.

Children's Groups

Children with disability should be welcomed to the Sunday school or children's groups so that they can enjoy learning and mixing with other children. There might need to be some flexibility regarding activities. Perhaps a child will find running or dancing difficult, but encourage the child to do the best he or she can. It is important to encourage the Sunday school teachers to learn a little about disability, as this will help them in planning activities.

We All Have Gifts to Share

God has blessed the church with spiritual gifts; he excludes no one from his generosity. In 1 Corinthians 12:7 Paul writes, "Now to each one the manifestation of the Spirit is given for the common good." God has given *each one* a gift to be used in the building up of his church. Paul does not say "each able-bodied person" but "*each one.*" This is inclusive language. Paul then lists a number of gifts, after which he writes, "All these [gifts] are the work of one and the same Spirit, and he distributes them to each one, just as he determines" (12:11).

Some people with disability will be more active than others, but God does not prevent anyone from receiving his gifts. How these different gifts are used will depend on the level of the person's ability, but every gift is useful to Christ and in the church.

How Can These Gifts Be Used in the Church?

The following are practical ideas for including the gifts of people with disability in the life of the church:

- Someone who has limited mobility can be welcomed to read the Scripture passage in the service. If they are a wheelchair-user, they can face the congregation from the front but at ground level, instead of using the lectern. If they are unable to stand for long, place a chair facing the congregation so they can sit to read the Scripture passage.
- A person with disability may have much to offer the church as a church elder or in some other leadership role. Look for the ability and not the disability.
- The choir or music group plays an important part in the service, leading people in praise to God or drawing them closer to God in repentance. Frequently the choir performs dance movements with the singing. Someone living with disability might be gifted by God with a beautiful voice. Will you deny that person the opportunity to use his or her gift because of an inability to dance? This person's gift is from God, and it is right for us to celebrate with them the gift they have been given.
- Helping with the offertory may be something that a child with intellectual impairment could do. The child could be assisted and guided by an adult; the family will feel great pride to see their child having a role to play in the service.

Figure 19.1. Young women with disabilities singing in the church choir.
Photo ©Bridget Hathaway.

- A clean church shows respect to God and the congregation. Many churches have a rota of people who clean the church. A person with intellectual impairment can be part of that rota, joining with others who can guide him or her in the cleaning tasks.
- If you have a welcome team, someone with a disability can be part of the team; it is not necessary to have mobility to welcome someone to church! The welcoming smile of someone with intellectual impairment can bring joy to those entering the building.
- The church leadership could appoint someone as accessibility officer for the church. This could be a member of the Mothers' Union.

Summary

As we have been reminded, the apostle Paul, in 1 Corinthians 12, describes the church as the body of Christ. The human body is fragile, susceptible to difficulties and imperfect. If we take this picture literally, then the church as the body of Christ is frail, vulnerable and open to impairments.

We need to seek the image of God in each person rather than focus on the impairment, the difference from what the world has deemed to be "normal."

Therefore, if the church as the body of Christ is to be inclusive, necessarily it must include people with impairment, otherwise it is not following Christ's teaching.

Case Study

Adam suffers from muscular dystrophy; we have known him for many years, having advocated on his behalf to enable him to gain a place at a government boarding primary school when he was no longer able to walk the long distance to his local school. He is now a young man, confined to his home and unable to lift his arms more than a few centimetres. The pastor of the local church invited him to be confirmed, along with a young man with intellectual impairment and many other young people. This was a great celebration, and a true example of inclusion in the church context. However, the story continues; the pastor and evangelist realized that Adam could not attend church, so they have arranged to hold a small communion service at Adam's home on a regular basis. Members of the church attend, and a church elder helps Mama Adam to prepare for the service. Praise God that in the years that he has left, Adam will be seen as part of the body of Christ!

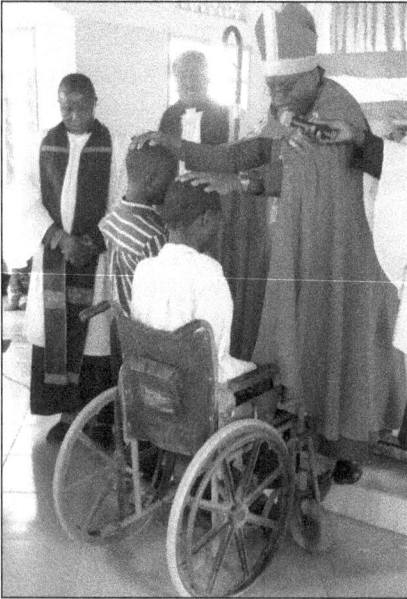

Figure 19.2. Adam receiving confirmation from Bishop Darlington, Diocese of Kagera, Tanzania. Photo ©Bridget Hathaway. Used by permission.

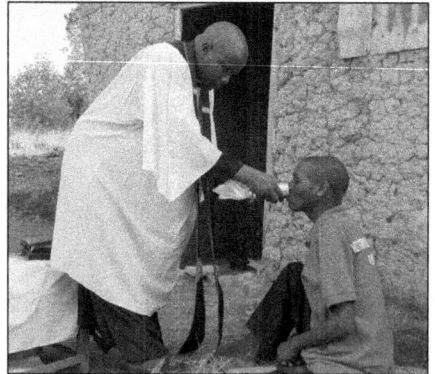

Figure 19.3. Adam receiving holy communion from Rev Canon Naftal Hosea at a service at his home. Photo ©Bridget Hathaway. Used by permission.

Bibliography

Adeyemo, Tokunboh, ed. *Africa Bible Commentary*. Nairobi: Word Alive; Grand Rapids, MI: Zondervan, 2006.

Bird, Anthony. *The Search for Health: A Response from the Inner City*. University of Birmingham, Institute for the Study of Worship and Religious Architecture, 1982.

Block, Jennie Weiss. *Copious Hosting*. New York: Continuum, 2002.

Bridger, Francis. *23 Days: A Story of Love, Death and God*. London: Darton, Longman & Todd, 2004.

Carson, D. A. *How Long, O Lord? Reflections on Suffering and Evil*. Nottingham: Inter-Varsity Press, 2006.

Creamer, Deborah Beth. *Disability and Christian Theology. Embodied Limits and Constructive Possibilities*. New York: Oxford University Press, 2009.

Eiesland, Nancy L. *The Disabled God: Towards a Liberatory Theology of Disability*. Nashville, TN: Abingdon, 1994.

Eiesland, Nancy L., and Don Saliers, eds. *Human Disability and the Service of God*. Nashville, TN: Abingdon, 1998.

Harshaw, Jill. *God beyond Words: Christian Theology and the Spiritual Experiences of People with Profound Intellectual Disabilities*. London; Philadelphia: Jessica Kingsley Publishers, 2016.

Haslam, Molly C. *A Constructive Theology of Intellectual Disability*. New York: Fordham University Press, 2012.

Hull, John M. *Disability: The Inclusive Church Resource*. London: Darton, Longman & Todd, 2014.

Kushner, Harold S. *When Bad Things Happen to Good People*. London: Pan Books, 1982.

Lo, Alison. *Encounter with God* (Bible Notes), 13 July 2018. Milton Keynes: Scripture Union, 2018.

Manchala, Deenabandhu. "Moving in the Spirit: Called to Transforming Discipleship." *International Review of Mission* 106, no. 2 (December 2017): 201–215.

Mandela, Nelson. *Long Walk to Freedom*. Boston: Little, Brown and Company, 1995.

Marshall, Alfred. *The NIV Interlinear Greek–English New Testament*. Grand Rapids, MI: Zondervan, 1976.

McCloughry, Roy. *The Enabled Life: Christianity in a Disabling World*. London: SPCK, 2013.

———. *Making a World of Difference*. London: SPCK, 2002.

McKeown, James. *Genesis*. Two Horizons Old Testament Commentary. Grand Rapids, MI: Eerdmans, 2008.

Molsberry, Robert F. *Blindsided by Grace: Entering the World of Disability*. Minneapolis, MN: Augsburg Fortress, 2004.

Pailin, David A. *A Gentle Touch: From a Theology of Handicap to a Theology of Human Being*. London: SPCK, 1992.

Pearsall, Judy, and Patrick Hanks, eds. *The New Oxford Dictionary of English*. Oxford: Oxford University Press, 1998.

Phelps-Jones, Tony. *Making Church Accessible to All: Including Disabled People in Church Life*. Abingdon: Bible Reading Fellowship, 2013.

Placher, William C. *Narratives of a Vulnerable God: Christ, Theology, and Scripture*. Louisville, KY: Westminster John Knox Press, 1994.

Rajkumar, Christopher, ed. *Sprouts of Disability Theology*. Nagpur, India: National Council of Churches in India, 2012.

Röhr-Rouendaal, Petra. *Where There Is No Artist*. Rugby: Practical Action, 2007.

Tataryn, Myroslaw, and Maria Truchan-Tataryn. *Discovering Trinity in Disability*. New York: Orbis, 2013.

Tournier, Paul. *What's in a Name?* London: SCM Press, 1975.

Wenham, Gordon. *Genesis 16–50*. Word Biblical Commentary. Dallas: Word, 1994.

Williams, Rowan. *Being Human: Bodies, Minds, Persons*. London: SPCK, 2018.

Wilson, Andrew, and Rachel Wilson. *The Life You Never Expected*. Nottingham: Inter-Varsity Press, 2015.

Wright, Tom. *John for Everyone: Part 1, Chapters 1–10*. London: SPCK; Louisville, KY: Westminster John Knox Press, 2002.

Yong, Amos. *The Bible, Disability and the Church*. Grand Rapids, MI: Eerdmans, 2011.

Young, Frances. *Arthur's Call*. London: SPCK, 2014.

Young, Frances, ed. *Encounter with Mystery: Reflections on L'Arche and Living with Disability*. London: Darton, Longman & Todd, 1997.

Langham Partnership is a global fellowship working in pursuit of the vision God entrusted to its founder John Stott –

> *to facilitate the growth of the church in maturity and Christ-likeness through raising the standards of biblical preaching and teaching.*

Our vision is to see churches in the majority world equipped for mission and growing to maturity in Christ through the ministry of pastors and leaders who believe, teach and live by the Word of God.

Our mission is to strengthen the ministry of the Word of God through:

- nurturing national movements for biblical preaching
- fostering the creation and distribution of evangelical literature
- enhancing evangelical theological education

especially in countries where churches are under-resourced.

Our ministry

Langham Preaching partners with national leaders to nurture indigenous biblical preaching movements for pastors and lay preachers all around the world. With the support of a team of trainers from many countries, a multi-level programme of seminars provides practical training, and is followed by a programme for training local facilitators. Local preachers' groups and national and regional networks ensure continuity and ongoing development, seeking to build vigorous movements committed to Bible exposition.

Langham Literature provides majority world preachers, scholars and seminary libraries with evangelical books and electronic resources through publishing and distribution, grants and discounts. The programme also fosters the creation of indigenous evangelical books in many languages, through writer's grants, strengthening local evangelical publishing houses, and investment in major regional literature projects, such as one volume Bible commentaries like *The Africa Bible Commentary* and *The South Asia Bible Commentary*.

Langham Scholars provides financial support for evangelical doctoral students from the majority world so that, when they return home, they may train pastors and other Christian leaders with sound, biblical and theological teaching. This programme equips those who equip others. Langham Scholars also works in partnership with majority world seminaries in strengthening evangelical theological education. A growing number of Langham Scholars study in high quality doctoral programmes in the majority world itself. As well as teaching the next generation of pastors, graduated Langham Scholars exercise significant influence through their writing and leadership.

To learn more about Langham Partnership and the work we do visit **langham.org**